RAND NATIONAL DEFENSE RESEARCH INSTITUTE

Authorities and Options for Funding USSOCOM Operations

Elvira N. Loredo, John E. Peters, Karlyn D. Stanley, Matthew E. Boyer, William Welser IV, Thomas S. Szayna

Prepared for the U.S. Special Operations Command
Approved for public release; distribution unlimited

This research was sponsored by USSOCOM and conducted within the International Security and Defense Policy Center of the RAND National Defense Research Institute, a federally funded research and development center sponsored by the Office of the Secretary of Defense, the Joint Staff, the Unified Combatant Commands, the Navy, the Marine Corps, the defense agencies, and the defense Intelligence Community.

Library of Congress Cataloging-in-Publication Data

ISBN: 978-0-8330-8506-1

Preface

Requirements to deploy Special Operations Forces (SOF) often arise unexpectedly, and they present complexity and limited flexibility of funding, which affect the ability of the various SOF commands to respond in a timely manner.

This report examines funding mechanisms, funding sources, and inter-Service agreements and develops recommendations that will reduce the frequency and duration of disputes between the U.S. Special Operations Command (USSOCOM), the Military Departments (MILDEPs), and Geographic Combatant Commands (GCCs) over their respective funding responsibilities for SOF, especially the use of Major Force Program 2 (MFP-2) and Major Force Program 11 (MFP-11) funds.

In exploring these issues and developing recommendations, the research team sought the perspectives of the Office of the Secretary of Defense, the individual MILDEPs, and GCC staffs. We were not able to consult with all of the parties involved in the funding process, however, so this report focuses on identifying areas where USSOCOM can improve its own internal fund management processes and areas of opportunity for dialogue with the MILDEPs on how to better coordinate the funding and resourcing of validated missions in support of the GCCs.

Implementation of the recommendations in this report will require close coordination between USSOCOM and the Under Secretary of Defense (Comptroller), the Assistant Secretary of Defense for Special Operations/Low-Intensity Conflict and Interdependent Capabilities, elements of the MILDEPs, U.S. Central Command, and the GCCs. In the process of that coordination, important fiscal policy, as well as resource allocation issues, will need to be resolved.

This research was sponsored by USSOCOM and conducted within the International Security and Defense Policy Center of the RAND National Defense Research Institute, a federally funded research and development center sponsored by the Office of the Secretary of Defense, the Joint Staff, the Unified Combatant Commands, the Navy, the Marine Corps, the defense agencies, and the defense Intelligence Community.

For more information on the RAND International Security and Defense Policy Center, see http://www.rand.org/nsrd/ndri/centers/isdp.html or contact the director (contact information is provided on the web page).

Contents

Figures and Tables

Figures

Tables

In the current operational environment, the Theater Special Operations Command (TSOC) headquarters at each AOR is responsible for identifying the funding to support the GCCs' validated requirements for the use of SOF. In most cases, the TSOCs coordinate with the Combatant Command Support Agents (CCSAs) and, with the guidance of paragraph 4 of the Execute Order (EXORD), identify the appropriate funding sources. However, there are instances when the TSOCs and the CCSAs do not agree on those sources. These disputes generally arise when validated but unfunded or unbudgeted[2] requirements are involved.

In the past, these types of requirements have been modest in both size and number and have often been funded with the help of Overseas Contingency Operation (OCO) dollars or, when appropriate, Major Force Program 11 (MFP-11) dollars, which are controlled directly by USSOCOM. In some instances, however, funding has been less straightforward, leading to disputes between the TSOCs and the CCSAs, primarily over whether the requirement being funded is Service-common and appropriately funded using Major Force Program 2 (MFP-2) or is SOF-peculiar and appropriately funded using MFP-11.[3] The lack of a clearly defined dispute resolution process at the action-officer (AO) level, along with a lack of consistent standards on the appropriate application of funding sources, has led to protracted delays in the execution of validated but unfunded requirements.

While all the relevant stakeholders may agree that a mission should be initiated and an EXORD issued, unfunded requirements (UFRs) pose a special funding challenge to the TSOC staffs, which must plan the details of the mission and secure funding from a variety of possible funding vehicles, each with strictly defined restrictions on its use. This complexity is further aggravated by the idiosyncratic way in which the relationships between TSOC staff and their corresponding MILDEP component commands have evolved and the limitations of the financial expertise resident in the TSOC staff.

If the the GCCs are to be provided with SOF agile enough to respond to emerging threats and opportunities, as called out in the GSN concept, the financial policies and procedures must be aligned accordingly.

Conclusions and Recommendations

This study was undertaken to investigate whether funding difficulties could be relieved by making USSOCOM the CCSA for the TSOCs. DoD Directive (DoDD) 5100.03

---

[2]   In this document, the term *unfunded* is used to refer to both unprogrammed and unbudgeted requirements. Unprogrammed requirements are those that have emerged since the beginning of the current budget year; unbudgeted requirements are those that were known but priorities precluded their funding.

[3]   MFP-2 and MFP-11 are defined in detail in Appendix B.

makes clear that CCSA is a responsibility conferred on a MILDEP by the Secretary of Defense. USSOCOM is not a MILDEP but a combatant command—the type of organization that is supposed to be the recipient of CCSA goods and services, not the provider of them. Further, CCSA status would create circumstances under which USSOCOM would have to reimburse the share of the base operating expenses incurred by USSOCOM personnel distributed across installations operated by defense components. This would incur additional accounting costs to track, report, and reimburse the Service-common expenses and Base Operating Support involved. Finally, and most importantly, CCSA status would not eliminate disputes that USSOCOM has with the MILDEPs concerning whether MFP-2 or MFP-11 funds should be used to pay for goods and services essential to newly validated operations. However, the TSOCs are now assigned to USSOCOM,[4] a change in organizational alignment that presents the Commander of USSOCOM with an opportunity to examine the current funding process and pursue a course of action that anticipates and eliminates or shortens the duration of funding disputes and also provides for more flexible funding.

Our recommendations fall into three categories: (1) reducing the number and duration of funding disputes; (2) increasing USSOCOM's flexibility in funding validated but unfunded and/or unbudgeted requirements, dealing in part with appropriated fund augmentation; and (3) improving the Memoranda of Agreement (MOAs) between the Services and USSOCOM.

Recommendations 1 through 4 below could be implemented in the near term, while recommendation 5 may require changes in the funding process that will need further vetting before action is taken. Each recommendation is consistent with the intent of DoDD 5100.03.

---

[4] The GCCs retain operational control (OPCON), i.e., command authority that may be exercised by commanders at any echelon at or below the level of combatant command. OPCON is inherent in combatant command authority and may be delegated within the command. OPCON is the authority to perform those functions of command over subordinate forces involving organizing and employing commands and forces, assigning tasks, designating objectives, and giving authoritative direction necessary to accomplish the mission. OPCON includes authoritative direction over all aspects of military operations and joint training necessary to accomplish missions assigned to the command. OPCON should be exercised through the commanders of subordinate organizations. Normally, this authority is exercised through subordinate joint force commanders and Service and/or functional component commanders. OPCON normally provides full authority to organize commands and forces and to employ those forces as the commander in OPCON considers necessary to accomplish assigned missions; it does not, in and of itself, include authoritative direction for logistics or matters of administration, discipline, internal organization, or unit training (Joint Publication 1-02, *DOD Dictionary of Military and Associated Terms*, November 8, 2010, as amended through June 15, 2013).

Reducing Funding Disputes

1.   USSOCOM should incorporate a financial planning element into the existing Rehearsal of Concept drill. Specifically, USSOCOM should expand the Rehearsal of Concept drill and synchronize it with the budget planning process to link potential funding sources, the responsibilities for funding, and the flow of funding to the requirements generated. This should include an identification of mission elements where congressional appropriation language may represent a hurdle to desired funding.

2.   DoDD 5100.03 establishes a high-level dispute resolution process intended to reduce the frequency and duration of funding disputes. At lower levels and consistent with the intent of the directive, USSOCOM should improve the ability of the CCSAs, GCCs, and MILDEP component commands to distinguish between Service-common (MFP-2) and SOF-peculiar (MFP-11) expenses and to resolve disputes expeditiously.

3.   To address the issues associated with financial planning, especially for validated but unfunded USSOCOM initiatives and operations, USSOCOM should establish J-8[5] as the center of expertise at USSOCOM Headquarters (HQ) responsible for shepherding the TSOCs through the requirements determination and funding process. The center should have expertise in multiple funding sources, should oversee the TSOCs' requirements determination process to ensure the applicability of funding, and should be able to draft Deployment Orders and Execute Orders with the required level of specificity to reduce ambiguity on the part of the Comptrollers and Contract Officers with regard to funding sources.

4.   Establish a collaborative annual training program for the MILDEPs, TSOCs, Staff Judge Advocates, and USSOCOM HQ staff to inform all parties involved in funding decisions of their roles and responsibilities, the dispute resolution process, and the MOAs and possible issues introduced by new legislation or regulations.

Increasing Flexibility

5.   If the President and Congress agree to expand the use of SOF as implied by the GSN concept,[6] ensuring the effective employment of SOF will require increasing the flexibility of funding for unfunded operations. We recommend that

---

[5]   J-8 is the Joint Staff Directorate for Force Structure, Resource, and Assessment (Department of Defense, 2010).

[6]   Under the GSN, SOF could increasingly be the tool of choice for more missions, and they would be geographically positioned to carry out more missions, which implies their increased use. If the President and Congress move forward with an expanded use of SOF as implied under the GSN, then increased funding flexibility would allow for a more effective and efficient employment of these capabilities.

USSOCOM and the MILDEPs pursue one of the following options with the Under Secretary of Defense (Comptroller):[7]

Option A. Request that the Office of the Secretary of Defense (OSD) work with Congress to authorize a SOF support Central Transfer Account (CTA) that would take the form of a single line-item appropriation similar to the counternarcotics CTA (Program Budget Decision 678, 1989). The SOF support CTA would be managed by the Assistant Secretary of Defense for Special Operations/Low-Intensity Conflict (ASD SO/LIC) to fund validated, unfunded SOF support requirements. The MILDEPs, GCCs, and Service component commands would be allocated resources by ASD SO/LIC from the fund to support validated SOF initiatives in their respective AORs.

Option B. USSOCOM could request authority from the Office of the Secretary of Defense to use MFP-11 to fund all validated requirements for emergency operations during the initial start-up phase, with the ultimate funding responsibility to be determined at a later date through the normal functional transfer and resource allocation processes.

Option C. Have the MILDEPs establish a flexible operating account using existing Operations and Maintenance funds to anticipate emergent SOF support funding requirements. The MILDEPs have some flexibility to make "fact of life" adjustments to the baseline budget. A forecast of SOF funding requirements, along with the GCC's priorities for those requirements, could establish the baseline flexible operating account. Funds to support this account could be administered by the MILDEPs, based on the GCC's priorities and in accordance with the regulations governing transfers within Operations and Maintenance accounts.

Any of these options would enable DoD to have flexible SOF to react quickly to emergency demands, while providing the time to build the unforeseen requirement into their Program Objective Memorandum and budget or, if necessary, seek supplemental funding. All options require a USSOCOM HQ center of expertise to manage the funding, budgeting, and execution, as well as the implementation of a dispute resolution structure and clearer definitions of MFP-2 and MFP-11 in the MOAs.

---

[7] For example, some type of revolving account might be established to anticipate unfunded requirements for SOF. Although no such mechanism is currently in place, a revolving account could be established by law. To establish one, it would be necessary to define and document the SOF requirements it would cover, establish a cost structure, and explore the legal ramifications and potential regulatory and legislative changes that would be required. Exploring the details of a revolving fund is beyond the scope of this research; however, a revolving fund could provide a solution to the underlying issue with funding flexibility identified here.

Abbreviations

AAO	Authorized Acquisition Objective
AF	Air Force
AF/CVA	Assistant Vice Chief of Staff of the Air Force
AFSOC	Air Force Special Operations Command
AOR	Area of Responsibility
ARSOF	Army Special Operations Forces
ASB	United States Army–United States Special Operations Command Board
ASD SO/LIC	Assistant Secretary of Defense for Special Operations/ Low-Intensity Conflict
BASOPS	base operations
BOS	Base Operating Support
CCSA	Combatant Command Support Agent
CDRUSSOCOM	Commander, United States Special Operations Command
CERP	Commander's Emergency Response Program
COCOM	Combatant Command
CRE	Crisis Response Element
CTA	Central Transfer Account
DoD	Department of Defense
DoDD	Department of Defense Directive
DON	Department of the Navy
DSG	Defense Strategic Guidance
EXORD	Execute Order/Executive Order
FRAGO	Fragmentary Order

FY	Fiscal Year
FYDP	Future Years Defense Program
GCC	Geographic Combatant Command
GPF	General Purpose Force
GSN	Global SOF Network
HQ	Headquarters
J-3	Operations Directorate of a Joint Staff
J-5	Plans Directorate of a Joint Staff
J-8	Force Structure, Resource, and Assessment Directorate of a Joint Staff
JCS	U.S. Joint Chiefs of Staff
JUONS	Joint Urgent Operational Needs Statement
MBI	Major Budget Issue
MFP-2	Major Force Program 2
MFP-11	Major Force Program 11
MILDEP	Military Department
MOA	Memoranda of Agreement
NAVCENT	U.S. Naval Forces Central Command
NAVSPECWARCOM	U.S. Naval Special Warfare Command
O&M	Operations and Maintenance
OCO	Overseas Contingency Operations
ONS	Operational Needs Statement
OPCON	Operational Control
OSD	Office of the Secretary of Defense
OSD(C)	Office of the Secretary of Defense (Comptroller)
PBD	Program Budget Decision
POM	Program Objective Memorandum
PPB	Planning, Programming, and Budgeting
PSC	Private Security Contractor
RIST	Resource Issue Support Team
SAF/AA	Secretary of the Air Force Administrative Assistant
SJA	Staff Judge Advocate

SOF	Special Operations Forces
SOR	Statement of Requirements
SPOC	Single Point of Contact
TSOC	Theater Special Operations Command
UFR	Unfunded Requirement
USAREUR	United States Army, European Command
USASOC	United States Army Special Operations Command
USD(C)	Under Secretary of Defense (Comptroller)
USEUCOM	United States European Command
USMC	United States Marine Corps
USN	United States Navy
USSOCOM	United States Special Operations Command

If approved, USSOCOM's GSN concept comprises three main elements:

1. Improve the special operations capabilities available to the Geographic Combatant Commands (GCCs) by augmenting the Theater Special Operation Command (TSOC) resources, capabilities, authorities, and force structure.
2. Ensure that DoD policies and authorities enable USSOCOM to be effective as a functional combatant command with global responsibilities.
3. In collaboration with U.S. interagency partners, build and employ a GSN that is enhanced and strengthened with willing and capable partner-nation SOF.

The GSN concept is intended to raise the role of SOF in the U.S. global posture and represents an ambitious long-term vision of SOF and their role in protecting U.S. interests. It emphasizes the strengths of SOF in supporting the objectives of GCCs in their respective Areas of Responsibility (AORs). In accordance with the DSG, a key attribute is the ability of SOF to gain situational awareness and build the capabilities of local forces, with a small footprint[4] and at a low cost (relative to the cost of general-purpose forces).

It is likely that the GCCs, in accordance with guidance received from the President and the Secretary of Defense, will generate requests for unplanned activities and operations, some of which will be in response to unanticipated events. Such events by definition fall outside of planned and programmed activities. It will fall to the TSOCs not only to plan operational support requirements in response to validated unfunded and/or unbudgeted (referred to as unfunded)[5] requirements but also to negotiate with a variety of stakeholders to secure the funding necessary to execute them. The principal problems addressed in this report concern disputes over institutional responsibility to pay; complexity, both in resolving disputes and in securing appropriate funding; and the tension between congressional appropriations on one hand and the availability of funding for the tasks at hand on the other. The disputes are often based on complex issues of law and administrative practices that are not well understood at various points in the decision process and that seem to loom throughout the process, beginning with the Statement of Requirements drafted by the TSOC. The Statement of Requirements identifies both SOF-peculiar and Service-common requirements to support the operation being planned. These requirements are validated through normal staff processes. In principle, USSOCOM is responsible for the SOF-peculiar goods and services, and the Service or its Service component com-

---

[4]   Department of Defense, 2012.

[5]   In this report, *unfunded* refers to both unprogrammed or unbudgeted requirements. Unprogrammed requirements are those that have emerged since the beginning of the current budget year; unbudgeted requirements are those that were known but priorities precluded their funding.

mand (or several of them) is tasked with providing funding for Service-common support, including base operating support (BOS). The taskings are staffed carefully, and the Military Departments (MILDEPs) or component commands play integral roles in the staffing and may ultimately "chop" (concur) on the taskings. However, funding disputes may arise even after "chopping" on the details of funding, and headquarters (HQ) may push back. At that point, staff officers try to resolve the impasse. When they fail to do so, the matter escalates to the Under Secretary of Defense (Comptroller) [USD(C)], where it is decided; the Office of the Secretary of Defense (OSD) then directs the manner for funding the required goods and services. This study presents potential options for reducing dispute numbers and duration.

History of Theater Special Operations Commands

This section describes the origins and evolution of the TSOCs,[6] how their funding evolved, and the current state of such funding.

Origins of the TSOCs

The TSOCs evolved idiosyncratically, although along similar trajectories. Several began as the Special Operations divisions of the theater J-3,[7] but most developed from standing task forces (e.g., Joint Unconventional Warfare Task Forces) and became functional component commands beginning in 1983; they then became subunified commands of their GCCs in 1986.[8] Variances in developmental paths, differences in staff capabilities along the way, and the quality of relationships with their parent commands affected the planning, programming, and budgeting (PPB) capabilities that eventually developed within the individual TSOCs.[9] In turn, these command relationships and capabilities have shaped the TSOCs' operational awareness and influence over their financial situation.

On April 16, 1987, USSOCOM was established as a unified combatant command pursuant to Pub. L. No. 99-443 and as directed by a Joint Chiefs of Staff (JCS) message, JCS Msg 142324Z Apr 87.[10] Under 10 U.S.C. § 167, USSOCOM was assigned several responsibilities and authorities, including the development and acquisition of

---

[6] We refer to these organizations as TSOCs throughout, although in 1989, they were still primarily Special Operations Divisions or task forces.

[7] Chairman, Joint Chiefs of Staff Instruction 4320.01, Enclosure A, paragraph 1(a).

[8] CAPT Mike Jones, "Theater Special Operations Command Resourcing," TSOC Desk Officer briefing, USSOCOM, undated.

[9] Wayne W. Anderson, Jr., *Alternative Headquarters Support Funding for Theater Special Operations Commands*, Monterey, Calif.: Naval Postgraduate School, thesis, December 2002.

[10] Jones, undated.

SOF-peculiar equipment and the acquisition of SOF-peculiar materials, supplies, and services. In August 1987, the Secretary of Defense issued a message reorganizing the SOF.[11] After that date, the Service Special Operations Commands would be resubordinated to USSOCOM. However, the TSOCs remained subordinated to their respective GCCs.

Evolution of TSOC Funding

Originally, since the TSOCs were constituent parts of the GCCs' staffs, the operating costs were paid by their theater combatant commands. With the creation of USSOCOM and the development of the TSOCs as subunified commands, funding provisions evolved.

Before November 1989, all SOF funding—Major Force Program 11 (MFP-11) and other funding—was included in the MILDEP budgets. This funding provided for the support of USSOCOM and its subordinate commands (e.g., the United States Army Special Operations Command [USASOC], the Air Force Special Operations Command [AFSOC], and the United States Naval Special Warfare Command [NAVSPECWARCOM]). No MFP-11 funding was allocated for the TSOCs.

With the promulgation of Program Budget Decision (PBD) 731C in December 1989, control of baseline MFP-11 funding moved from the MILDEPs to USSOCOM. Service-common and BOS funding were not included in this functional transfer, nor was funding for the TSOCs. Next, a Defense Conference Report effective in fiscal year (FY) 1992 pursuant to Pub. L. 102-190, National Defense Authorization Act for Fiscal Years 1992 and 1993, moved all funding associated with the TSOCs to MFP-11.[12] A memo from the Assistant Secretary of Defense for Special Operations/Low-Intensity Conflict (ASD SO/LIC) directed that funding arrangements for the TSOCs not be different from those for funding other SOF commands with MFP-11 dollars.[13] The arrangement that prevails today thus took shape: MFP-11 funds are controlled by HQ USSOCOM and used for its subordinated Service-component HQ activities (AFSOC, USASOC, NAVSPECWARCOM). Funding for goods, services, and activities that are not SOF-peculiar was to be provided by MILDEP executive agents, the forerunner of today's combatant command support activities. Several more modifications to funding procedures occurred—PBD 623 (FY 1993), PBD 744 (FY 1994), USD(C) Memo directing implementation of the Planning, Budgeting and Adminis-

---

[11] SECDEF msg 241808Z Feb 87, "Reorganization of DoD Special Operations," in Jones, undated. The message identified service component commands assigned to USSOCOM as USASOC, AFSOC, and Naval Special Warfare Command. Joint Special Operations Command was reassigned in a separate message.

[12] U.S. Congress, Defense Conference Report, H. Rept. 102-311, 1991.

[13] Assistant Secretary of Defense for Special Operations/Low-Intensity Conflict and Interdependent Capabilities, ASD SO/LIC Memo, July 10, 1992.

trative System[14]—but none of them transferred responsibility or authority for funding Service-common and BOS goods and services from the MILDEPs to USSOCOM; to do otherwise would have made Service-common and BOS reimbursement arrangements more complicated and more expensive by requiring USSOCOM to account for and reimburse them on an installation-by-installation basis.

On December 19, 2000, PBD 081 was issued, confirming the responsibilities of the MILDEPs to fund Service-common and BOS requirements and closing loopholes in the use of MFP-11 funds that had begun to emerge. It directed that DoD Directive (DoDD) 5100.3 be amended to reflect that the source of funding for TSOC direct HQ support would be the supporting MILDEP. Provision of adequate funding was the responsibility of the GCC to which the TSOC was assigned. Table 1.1 summarizes the primary directives and their impacts.

The PDB also directed USSOCOM to transfer $2.5 million per year to the Services from MFP-11 through the Future Years Defense Program (FYDP) to support the TSOCs, because the TSOCs had used MFP-11 funds to pay for common support requirements.

Table 1.1
Program Budget Decisions and Other Directives and Their Effects on USSOCOM Funding

Date	Action/Circumstance	Outcome
Pre–November 1989	MFP-11 and other SOF funding placed in MILDEP budgets	None allocated for TSOCs
December 1989	PBD 731C moves MFP-11 funds from MILDEPs to USSOCOM. Service-common funds and BOS remain with MILDEPs	None allocated to TSOCs
December 1992	PBD 623	Funding for TSOC SOF-peculiar requirements in FY 1993 budget
March 1993	PBD 744	MFP-11 funds allocated to TSOCs for SOF-peculiar requirements for FY 1994–FY 1999
February 1996	Under Secretary of Defense (Comptroller) memo directs all DoD funds to be issued and controlled through Program Budget and Accounting System	TSOCs receive direct distribution of MFP-11 funds for SOF-peculiar requirements in FY 1997
December 2000	PBD 081 directs that the MILDEP responsible for supporting a GCC is also responsible for TSOC HQ support (but does not direct a specific funding pathway)	USSOCOM directs a stop to use of MFP-11 funding for TSOC HQ suport. PBD realigns MFP-11 and MFP-2 funds in accordance with a recent audit
February 2001	USSOCOM memo directs each TSOC to work with its respective GCC resourcing program to obtain support needed to operate the TSOC HQ	

---

[14] Under Secretary of Defense (Comptroller) Memorandum, February 9, 1996.

eral definition of MOAs and their functions and reviews and critiques three of the MOAs between USSOCOM and the MILDEPs. It also offers examples of other MOAs between DoD and other U.S. government entities. Appendix B discusses some important funding sources that are or have been available for USSOCOM operations. It provides an overview of the U.S. Defense Program and MFP-2 and MFP-11, and it describes types of funding, the sources of the funds, and the limitations on their use.

CHAPTER TWO

Challenges and Issues Concerning TSOC Funding

Should USSOCOM Become the CCSA of the TSOCs?

We first considered whether the funding challenges posed by USSOCOM's validated but unfunded requirements might be resolved by USSOCOM obtaining CCSA status. DoDD 5100.03 defines CCSA as

> The Secretary of a Military Department to whom the Secretary of Defense or the Deputy Secretary of Defense has assigned administrative and logistical support of the headquarters of a combatant command, United States Element, North American Aerospace Defense Command, or subordinate unified command. The nature and scope of the combatant command support agent responsibilities, functions, and authorities shall be prescribed at the time of assignment or in keeping with existing agreements and practices, and they shall remain in effect until the Secretary of Defense or the Deputy Secretary of Defense revokes, supersedes, or modifies them.

As DoDD 5100.03 makes clear, CCSA is a responsibility conferred on a MILDEP by the Secretary of Defense. USSOCOM is not a MILDEP; it is a combatant command, the type of organization that is supposed to be the recipient of CCSA goods and services, not the provider of them. Having CCSA status would create circumstances under which USSOCOM would have to reimburse its share of the base operating expenses incurred by USSOCOM personnel distributed across installations operated by defense components. Doing so would cause USSOCOM and the defense components to incur additional accounting costs to track, report, and reimburse the Service-common expenses and BOS involved. Finally, and most importantly, CCSA status would not eliminate disputes that USSOCOM has with the MILDEPs concerning whether MFP-2 or MFP-11 funds should be used to pay for goods and services for newly validated operations. Since CCSA authority does not resolve the fundamental source of the disputes—whether the expense in question is SOF-peculiar or Service-common—conferring such status on USSOCOM has the unintended potential of further complicating such disputes. Therefore, we discarded the idea of USSOCOM obtaining CCSA status. The following section examines the key issues faced by the TSOCs in supporting USSOCOM's operations.

Scope of the TSOC Funding Issue

At first glance, it might appear that UFRs would be a reliable measure of the magnitude of the funding problems the TSOCs are encountering. Figure 2.1 presents the recent history of UFRs in MFP-2 and MFP-11. The UFRs are fairly modest in size, amounting to less than 0.5 percent of the USSOCOM Operations and Maintenance (O&M) budget for FY 2011.[1]

However, the UFRs reflect shortfalls only in known requirements (as opposed to unfunded requirements)—goods and services considered as the budget was being formulated that fell short of the cut line, given the priorities driving the budget-building process. In this regard, UFRs reflect the type of trade-offs confronting most commands. Some of these trade-offs involve risk, although we encountered very few that involved force protection or other significant risks.

Figure 2.1
TSOCs' Recent History of Unfinanced Requirements

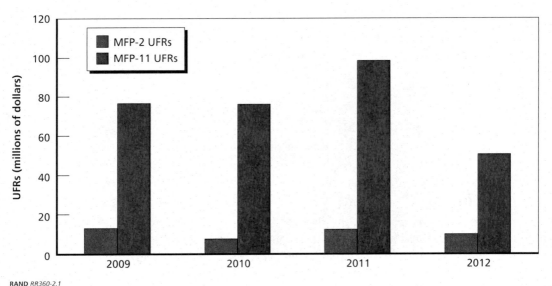

RAND RR360-2.1

_____
[1]   United States Special Operations Command Operations and Maintenance, Defense-Wide Fiscal Year (FY) 2011 Budget Estimates.

These issues, however, do not capture the importance of unfunded requirements. And it is the unfunded requirements that lie at the heart of the funding disputes between USSOCOM, the MILDEPs and the combatant commands. These unfunded requirements make additional, unanticipated demands on the resources of the MILDEPs and the combatant commands. The decrease in Overseas Contingency Operations (OCO) funds has been a significant contributing factor to budget pressures generally and to the GCCs' ability to cope with TSOC unfunded operational support requirements.[2] The OCO funding was a significant source of elasticity in DoD funding and a key resource for satisfying unfunded requirements.[3] These OCO funds have declined in absolute terms approximately 44 percent from FY 2011 to FY 2013. In addition to the overall reduction in OCO, approximately 2 percent of the remaining funding has been consumed by cost increases (e.g., for fuel) and inflation, further decreasing the amount of OCO funding available. Finally, some OCO funding was moved into the regular MILDEP budget accounts, where the funds had to be spent in ways consistent with the specific budget lines—again reducing flexibility.

Figure 2.2 illustrates the effects of price and program growth on the MILDEP O&M budgets from FY 2011 through FY 2013.[4] Together with the reductions in OCO funding, these reductions limit the MILDEPs' flexibility in responding to unfunded TSOC operational support requirements by reducing elasticity within the O&M budget—there are simply fewer funds that might be reallocated. The FY 2011 reduction in program growth was across the board but was most significant for the Army, as its operations tempo slowed down in Operation New Dawn. Modest program growth (net of cost growth) appeared in FY 2013: $5,478.8 million for Army O&M, $2,300.6 million for Navy O&M, and –$1,202.0 million for Air Force O&M. The FY 2013 estimates represent modest increases over FY 2012 but clear declines from FY 2011, especially in the case of Army O&M.

Recent budget actions may have made funding disputes more frequent and acute, but the memoranda, briefings, and email exchanges we reviewed suggest that the same issues were present in 2006 and earlier, when funding was abundant. The small size of the MFP-2 UFRs suggests that MILDEP programming for known requirements works reasonably well. The issue with unfunded requirements appears to be independent of changes in funding availability. Availability is the area where the MILDEPs

---

[2] As discussed in Fiscal Year 2013 Budget Estimates, United States Special Operations Command Operations and Maintenance, Defense-Wide Fiscal Year (FY) 2013 Budget Estimates, pp. 355–357.

[3] OCO funding was originally geographically oriented toward Iraq, Afghanistan, the Horn of Africa, and the Philippines but was almost immediately expanded to authorize the use of funds at home station. Some programs funded by OCO, such as the Commander's Emergency Response Program (CERP), included fairly broad categories of activities and programs. The Government Accountability Office (GAO) encouraged DoD to enact closer controls on OCO. See, for example, GAO-10-288R, December 18, 2009.

[4] Based on data from p. 1 of Fiscal Year 2013 Budget Estimates, United States Special Operations Command Operations and Maintenance, Defense-Wide Fiscal Year (FY) 2013 Budget Estimates.

Figure 2.2
Price and Program Growth in MILDEP O&M Budgets

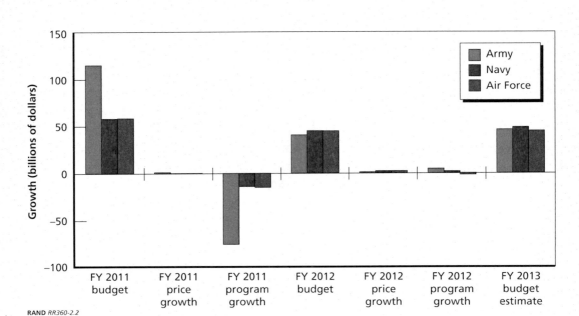

RAND *RR360-2.2*

struggle and will likely continue to face difficulties in accommodating the demand for financing of TSOC unfunded operational support during execution. Demand is the independent variable, mirroring the turbulence and dynamism in the international security environment and the GCCs' desire to treat the challenges that emerge with SOF.

Managing Unfunded Requirements

The difficulties associated with managing unfunded requirements are likely to persist. The MILDEPs' problem with respect to unfunded requirements may be made worse by the uncertain demands for the employment of SOF in support of the GCCs' campaign plans in their AORs. Future demands are likely to differ from historical trends, because they reflect not only perturbations in international security but also how the GCCs choose to employ SOF in their AORs, complicating MILDEP efforts to fund TSOC operational support requirements.

Challenges for TSOC Funding of Unfunded Requirements

USSOCOM faces broad funding challenges which are likely to become more acute if the main elements of the GSN concept are implemented. First, challenges stem from the organization and financial planning capabilities of the TSOCs and the limits to their ability to secure appropriate funding and manage disputes. Second, complexities arise from the many sources, authorities, and constraints and limitations imposed on DoD funding by the many layers of supervision, from Congress to the Office of Management and Budget, DoD, and the MILDEPs. The potential penalties faced by MILDEP officials in the event of a violation of statutory authority for the use of appropriated funds contribute heavily to the conduct of financial dispute resolution and are one of the bases for our recommendation on enhanced staff officer training.

Table 2.1 provides a summary of some of the funding sources available, in addition to MFP-2 and MFP-11 funding. The details of the provisions of the funding sources complicate the resolution of funding disputes. The sources are described in more detail in Appendix B.

Table 2.1
Potential Funding Sources

Fund	Purpose	Limitations
Global Security Contingency Fund (22 U.S.C. § 2151)	Provide assistance to countries designated by the Secretary of State, with the concurrence of the Secretary of Defense	Assistance may be provided only for activities that promote "observance of and respect for human rights and fundamental freedoms" and "respect for legitimate civilian authority" (22 U.S.C. § 2151(c)).
Cooperative Threat Reduction (50 U.S.C. § 2922)	Destroy chemical weapons in Shchuch'ye, Russia Prevent biological-weapons proliferation Allow the "acceleration, expansion, and strengthening of Cooperative Threat Reduction Program activities" (50 U.S.C. § 2922(b))	Appropriated funds "may not exceed the amounts authorized to be appropriated by any national defense authorization act for fiscal year 2008 to the Department of Defense Cooperative Threat Reduction Program for such purposes" (50 U.S.C. § 2922(a)); Congress requests that the President "accelerate and expand funding" for these programs in future years (50 U.S.C. § 2922(b)).
Emergency Extraordinary Expense Funds (10 U.S.C. § 127)	"Provide for any emergency or extraordinary expense which cannot be anticipated or classified" (10 U.S.C. § 127(a))	The Secretary of Defense must notify certain congressional committees and allow a certain period of time to pass, before spending more than $500,000. This requirement is waived if the Secretary of Defense determines that compliance will compromise national security objectives; however, he then must notify the committees immediately.

Table 2.1—Continued

Fund	Purpose	Limitations
Confidential Military Purpose Funds	Funds may be authorized without disclosing their purpose, provided the appropriate secretary or inspector general certifies that the expenditures are necessary for confidential military purposes	Limitations are substantively the same as those for Emergency Extraordinary Expense Funds. Additionally, the appropriate secretary or inspector general must certify that the expenditure is necessary for confidential military purposes.
Joint Combined Exchange Training (10 U.S.C. § 2011)	"The primary purpose of the training for which payment may be made . . . shall be to train the special operations forces of the combatant command" (10 U.S.C. § 2011(b))	The Secretary of Defense shall develop regulations related to this funding, including a requirement that funded activities must have the prior approval of the Secretary of Defense.
Combatant Commander Initiative Fund (10 U.S.C. § 166(a))	Force training, contingencies, selected operations, command and control, joint exercises, humanitarian assistance, etc.	Spending is limited to $20 million on items "with a unit cost in excess of the investment unit cost" (10 U.S.C. § 166a(e)) $10 million for expenses of foreign nations during joint exercises $5 million to provide military education and training to personnel of foreign countries. Funds may not be provided for "any activity that has been denied authorization by Congress."
Combating Terrorism Readiness Initiative Fund (10 U.S.C. § 166(b))	"(1) Procurement and maintenance of physical security equipment (2) Improvement of physical security sites (3) Under extraordinary circumstances (A) Physical security management planning (B) Procurement and support of security forces and security technicians (C) Security reviews and investigations and vulnerability assessments (D) Any other activity relating to physical security" (10 U.S.C. § 166b(b))	Funds may not be provided for "any activity that has been denied authorization by Congress." Priority should be given to "emergency or emergent unforeseen high-priority requirements for combating terrorism" (10 U.S.C. § 166b(c)).
Combat Mission Requirements Fund (10 U.S.C. § 167)		No limitations are listed, although there are extensive reporting requirements.

Table 2.1—Continued

Fund	Purpose	Limitations
Commander's Emergency Response Program	"Respond to urgent humanitarian relief and reconstruction requirements within [the commanders'] areas of responsibility, by carrying out programs that will immediately assist the Iraqi people and support the reconstruction of Iraq" (June 16, 2003, memo by Ambassador Paul Bremer)	Fragmentary Order (FRAGO) 89 prohibited expenditures for seven categories: • Direct or indirect benefit of Combined Joint Task Force 7 (CJTF-7) forces, to include coalition forces • Entertaining Iraqi population • Weapons buy-back or rewards programs • Buying firearms, ammunition, or removing unexploded ordnance • Duplicating services available through municipal governments • Supporting individuals or private businesses (exceptions possible, such as repairing damage caused by coalition forces) • Salaries for the civil work force, pensions, or emergency civil service worker payments (37 JFQ 46, 48). The amounts that may be spent (both per-transaction and in general) depend on the level of the commander authorizing the transaction.
Pub. L. 109-163 § 1206	"[T]o conduct or support a program to build the capacity of a foreign country's national military forces in order for that country to (1) conduct counterterrorist operations or (2) participate in or support military and stability operations in which the United States Armed Forces are a participant" (Pub. L. 109-163, § 1206(a))	The Secretary of Defense must have the concurrence of the Secretary of State. Funding is limited to $350 million and shall include elements that promote respect for human rights, fundamental freedoms, and legitimate civilian authority.
Pub. L. 108-375 § 1208	"[T]o provide support to foreign forces, groups, or individuals engaged in supporting or facilitating ongoing military operations by United States special operations forces to combat terrorism" (Pub. L. 108-375, § 1208(a))	Before spending funds, the Secretary must establish procedures and inform Congress of these provisions. This authority cannot be delegated. This does not "constitute authority to conduct a covert action" (Pub. L. 108-375, § 1208(e)).

The third challenge results from the financial planning limitations within the SOF enterprise—specifically, the deliberate budgeting process and the process for funding unfunded requirements, respectively. And fourth, USSOCOM and its subordinate offices do not adequately maintain, revise, and enforce their MOAs with the MILDEPs to ensure that they more clearly delineate the responsibilities of the Services and provide for expeditious dispute resolution.

Factors that complicate the funding of validated but unfunded requirements for the TSOCs include the following:

- TSOCs differ significantly in their organizations and capabilities.
- Many TSOC disputes with the MILDEPs concern MFP-2 or MFP-11 funding.

- The unfamiliar nature of SOF requirements leads to debate concerning BOS and Service-common support.
- There is a multitude of funding sources, authorities, and constraints.
- The SOF enterprise has a limited capacity for PPB.
- Omissions in the MOAs that USSOCOM has with the Services can create disputes and problems that ultimately can impact the effectiveness of USSOCOM's ability to support the GCCs.

TSOC Organizations and Capabilities Vary Significantly

The TSOCs have evolved idiosyncratically and do not share a common organization or set of authorities. One trait they do seem to share is that they are lean organizations without substantial expertise in operational funding. They have a limited capacity to carry out planning and coordination with their CCSAs, GCCs, and other defense component commands, although, in the case of Crisis Response Elements (CREs) (described later in this report), TSOC staff may have to negotiate with multiple organizations to secure funding for a single initiative. Officers assigned to the TSOC's J-8 are often in their first assignment to a headquarters command and are unfamiliar with the complexity of funding issues. Assigned personnel represent a mix of specialties, and there is no guarantee that they will have a background in finance or budgeting. Most uniformed personnel come from the general-purpose force, including the reserve component, and have limited financial planning and budgeting experience. This condition is likely to persist and presents an inherent limitation. The TSOCs' responsibilities also differ. Some prepare their own POMs, while others do not. Some have insight into the broader resource picture of the GCCs and the CCSA, while others have none. The nature of the relationship of a TSOC with the GCC varies from theater to theater and tends to reflect the circumstances under which the TSOC evolved into its present organizational state. For some, the relationship is formal, with the TSOCs engaged only on issues involving them directly. For others, the relationship is more collegial, with the GCC providing greater situational awareness of issues confronting the AOR to its TSOC.

Many TSOC Disputes with the Services Concern MFP-2 or MFP-11 Funding

The major features of SOF funding are the distinction between MFP-2 and MFP-11 and the special-purpose language of statutory authorities. MFP-11 was created to allow USSOCOM to pay for SOF-peculiar goods and services. Service-common goods and services and BOS are to be paid for with general-purpose force funds in MFP-2. As a practical matter, the distinctions between MFP-2 and MFP-11 are most important during programming and budgeting. Nevertheless, they endure in the minds of staff officers and officials at MILDEP and headquarters, in combatant command staffs, within the TSOCs, and at USSOCOM when the organizations are engaged in appropriation cognizance discussions, even though the funding that is actually available in the organizational budgets has lost these MFP-related tags by the time funds are appropriated. The notion persists that money from the Services is MFP-2 and meant for Service-common goods and services, while any funding from USSOCOM is MFP-11 and intended to buy SOF-peculiar goods and services. When overlaid with consideration of "special authority" language, the difficulties for fiscal officials can be appreciated. The funding disputes between USSOCOM and the MILDEPs primarily concern fundamental differences of interpretation about what constitutes Service-common and BOS on one hand and SOF-peculiar on the other. DoDD 5100.03 acknowledges that the definition of Service-common will vary depending on the MILDEP. Further, it establishes a DoD policy that "disputes concerning the support of these headquarters shall be elevated through the Chairman of the Joint Chiefs of Staff to the Secretary of Defense for resolution." However, although DoDD 5100.03 establishes responsibilities to resolve disputes, it does not establish a series of triggers starting at the action officer (AO) level that will identify and escalate disputes and encourage timely resolution. The absence of a well-defined dispute resolution process results in protracted administrative delays in establishing responsibility for funding and the raising of issues only when they have reached a crisis. This encourages a culture of crisis management that is not conducive to efficient execution of USSOCOM's GSN (if approved) or to flexible response operations.

The Unfamiliar Nature of SOF Requirements Creates Debate Concerning BOS and Service-Common Support

SOF operations and practices are often unfamiliar to MILDEP, CCSA, GCC, and defense component command comptrollers, financial managers, and contracting officials. For example, "unusual" requests for support (e.g., indigenously procured vehicles) are sometimes equated with being SOF-peculiar, while the USSOCOM considers them to be Service-common and not unique to SOF. Another example is the costs associated with building a boat dock. The dock itself had no attributes that rendered it SOF-peculiar, yet GCC officials argued it was an MFP-11 expense because Navy Special Warfare Boat Units would be using it and related that to authority to construct facilities. Officials have sometimes argued that facilities were SOF-peculiar and therefore should be operated with MFP-11 funds because there were no general-purpose forces on them—even though the general nature of the dining facility, billeting, and similar support were otherwise common needs across the MILDEP, i.e., Service-common. In some cases, a weapon can be both SOF-peculiar and Service-common. An M-4 carbine is Service-common for the Army, where it serves as a standard weapon in the infantry. In Navy Special Warfare organizations, however, it is SOF-peculiar because the Navy otherwise does not use M-4s; it uses M-16s instead and must procure M-4s specifically for its SOF element. Restrictions in appropriation bills may also come into play, complicating and limiting the MILDEPs' funding decisions. For example, appropriation bills often contain restrictions such as "Buy American" or numerical controls when it comes to vehicles. These are considerations that impact MILDEP considerations, as the MILDEPs are the holders of statutory responsibility. The distinctions between Service-common and SOF-peculiar are not straightforward, and officials therefore need guidelines and precedents to help them distinguish between these expenses.

The Multitude of Funding Sources, Authorities, and Constraints Creates Problems for the TSOCs in Funding Operations

TSOCs have access to a variety of funding sources. Their base budgets, which cover the operation of the TSOC headquarters and its BOS, are provided by the MILDEP designated the CCSA for the AOR in the form of MFP-2 funds. The funding is usually not provided directly to a TSOC but comes to it through the parent GCC.

Many special authorities make other funding available for specific activities or to address specific threats and military missions. Congress has included some of these (e.g., 1206, 1207, and 1208 funding) in annual Defense Appropriations Acts. Others, such as the Global Security Contingency Fund and the Commander's Emergency Response Program, have their origins in different legislation. Each of the special authorities comes with constraints that specify how the funds may be spent.

Interviews with TSOC staff members indicate that they often have difficulty managing funds that result from special authorities (e.g., 1208). The TSOC assignment is, for many AOs, the first job in which they have had to grapple with these types of funding issues, and many find the "color of money" issues confusing.

Another class of funding has emerged from U.S. operations in Iraq and Afghanistan. The largest part of this funding has been the separate OCO funding that Congress made available to finance those operations over and above the funding in the base budgets. Combat operations also spawned Operational Needs Statements (ONSs) and Joint Urgent Operational Needs Statements (JUONSs) that, when validated, could require funding to address a commander's urgent battlefield needs or address a newly discovered vulnerability.[5] SOF commanders have had access to both OCO and ONS/JOUNS-related funds. The availability of OCO funds has eased, and perhaps masked, some of the funding challenges faced by the TSOCs by providing an alternative funding source that was subject to fewer conditions and constraints. However, OCO funding is ebbing, and fewer forward locations qualify for the remaining OCO funds.

Specific challenges to the TSOCs' ability to fund operations include arranging funding across multiple headquarters and reaching consensus on funding responsibilities.

Arranging Funding Across Multiple Headquarters. Some new initiatives (e.g., the USSOCOM CREs) evolve without programmed funding, which, though not

---

[5] Policy for the management of the ONS and JUONS validation and funding process is given in DoDI 5000.02 and DoDD 5000.71.

unusual, nevertheless requires the TSOC staff to secure the funding to pay for them. TSOC staff often need to negotiate with representatives of the CCSA, the GCCs, and USSOCOM HQ. Depending on the complexity of the operation, multiple CCSAs may be involved.

Despite the multiple sources of funding for SOF operations, securing adequate support is often difficult. For example, a CRE is a validated operation seeking to take advantage of an emergent opportunity to cooperate with an important strategic partner. However, the location and mix of personnel involved in the CRE may require the coordination of funding responsibilities in the development of the Execute Order (EXORD). This may prove to be problematic, especially in the absence of a dispute resolution mechanism. The existence of multiple funding sources complicates matters, and AOs may devote weeks to resolving funding responsibilities. A review of CRE issues noted the following:

> Securing Service-common, to include BOS, support for SOF deployed forces continues to be a challenge which requires constant education and negotiation. As OCO funds and OCO-eligible locations become scarcer, these challenges will grow in magnitude. Early identification of the proper support providers in the planning stages is key to ensuring GCC Service Components can properly plan and budget for the support required for SOF operations. In this era of diminishing resources, conventional forces withdrawal and increased role of SOF forces in austere locations, it is imperative that USSOCOM, its Service Components, the TSOCs, and GCCs coordinate a multi-prong approach to ensure the Services are aware of and are able to fulfill their responsibility to support SOF as directed in Department guidance. (United States Special Operations Command, 2011)

Using a CRE example, Figure 2.3 illustrates the lengthy time lines involved in resolving funding for USSOCOM validated but unfunded requirements.

Reaching Consensus on Funding Responsibilities. Deliberate planning involving many stakeholders and headquarters (e.g., considering likely funding liabilities as the fiscal year ends and the first POM year becomes the new budget execution year) is complex, presenting many opportunities for misunderstandings and crossed signals. Regular Rehearsal of Concept drills that involve all stakeholders in the funding requirements that will emerge in the new budget year could reduce the likelihood of misunderstandings and disputes over funding responsibility.

The TSOCs Have Limited Capacity for Planning, Programming, and Budgeting

As is the case with most of the combatant commands, USSOCOM's PPB capability was designed primarily for deliberate operations, i.e., those defined by the annual budget cycle. The TSOCs possess uneven and sometimes quite limited capabilities in this area. The calendars of events that drive the MFP-2 and MFP-11 PPB processes are not completely synchronized and run out of phase with each other. As a result of these

Figure 2.3
Illustrative Time Line for Evolution of a CRE

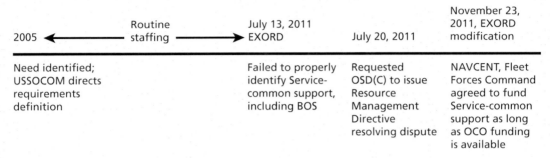

2005	Routine staffing →	July 13, 2011 EXORD	July 20, 2011	November 23, 2011, EXORD modification
Need identified; USSOCOM directs requirements definition		Failed to properly identify Service-common support, including BOS	Requested OSD(C) to issue Resource Management Directive resolving dispute	NAVCENT, Fleet Forces Command agreed to fund Service-common support as long as OCO funding is available

SOURCE: SOCCENT White Paper, December 30, 2011.
RAND *RR360-2.3*

circumstances, there is no robust process to harmonize and rationalize PPB across the SOF enterprise and its multiplicity of funding sources. The resulting challenges include those described in the rest of this section.

Challenges in Execution of the Deliberately Planned Budget. Challenges involved in executing the deliberately planned budget for the current fiscal year are described in the section above on the multitude of funding sources.

Challenges Associated with Validated, Unfunded Requirements. The operating characteristics of the current PPB system can lead to disputes between USSOCOM and potential bill payers. USSOCOM and its TSOCs may insist that the goods and services in question are legitimate MFP-2 Service-common and BOS expenses, while the potential bill payers, confronted with these unfunded requirements, will insist that they are SOF-peculiar. Therefore, staff practices and procedures are demanding when a TSOC staff must develop plans to execute emergent missions or operations. The staff must develop the entire concept of operations, vet it up the chain of command, and support it with requests for forces while simultaneously securing the funding for it. Because planning the actual activity or operation is inherently more attractive to the staff officers involved (they are usually expert at this), planning advances relatively quickly, while the search for funding lags. The planning also has a dynamic quality, so the Statement of Requirements (SOR) the AOs develop expands rather quickly. Often, CCSAs, GCCs, and defense component commands that may be responsible for funding all or part of the effort prefer to wait until the SOR has been finally validated before giving it serious attention. Ultimately, the SOR must be staffed and approved by all the stakeholders, including the organizations tasked to provide funding for the Service-common expenses and BOS. Even when all of the stakeholders have concurred with the EXORD, disputes about the expenses the individual stakeholders will pay for may develop subsequently as each of the stakeholders interprets its own liability very conservatively and assumes that others will be the major bill payers. In the CRE example, the EXORD had to be modified to readdress funding responsibilities.

Many staff officers find the process of securing funding onerous and look for expedient ways to secure the funds for required Service-common expenses and BOS. Frequently they rely on "boilerplate" language that has been used to describe funding relationships in earlier projects, which they then paste into paragraph 4 of EXORDs and Deployment Orders. In instances where the circumstances of the project or initiative are routine, the boilerplate can be effective. But in cases where the circumstances are unfamiliar to the responsible officers in the CCSA, GCC, or defense component command directed to provide the support, this general language does not withstand scrutiny, and a dispute over funding responsibilities ensues.

Challenges Associated with Unfinanced Requirements. TSOCs usually face validated but unfinanced requirements in both MFP-2 and MFP-11 funding and seek funding to cover these shortfalls. In the case of MFP-2, seeking funding means requesting additional funds from the CCSA or sometimes from the GCC. In most cases, the TSOC has to communicate using its chain of command, which flows through the GCC headquarters. In some instances, the TSOC approaches the CCSA through its local MILDEP component command (e.g., U.S. Army Europe in the case of U.S. European Command, whose CCSA is the Department of the Army). Even when the TSOC sustains its case and the CCSA determines that it will provide funding to address the MFP-2 unfinanced requirement, the intermediate headquarters through which the funding must pass can take actions that are not consistent with the CCSA's intent. These intermediate headquarters can retain part of the funding for their own use, and they can reprioritize so as to delay delivery of it to the TSOC until a later date. Confronted with such delays, TSOCs sometimes appeal to USSOCOM. In some instances, the United States Pacific Command has delayed delivering MFP-2 funding, and USSOCOM has provided MFP-11 funds. Theoretically, TSOCs are able to petition OSD for a Resource Board[6] action to provide essential funding. In practice, however, the TSOCs are not invited to represent their issues directly, and the matter is usually settled between the GCC and the CCSA.

Omissions in Current MOAs Can Create Disputes

Omissions in the MOAs that USSOCOM has with the MILDEPs can create disputes and problems that ultimately can impact USSOCOM's ability to provide support to

---

[6] As part of a process to resolve major budget issues (MBIs), the MILDEP Secretary and Service Chief meet with the Secretary of Defense and the Deputy Secretary of Defense. Once they make a decision (staff formulate recommendations ahead of the meeting), the OSD Comptroller issues a PBD or OSD Memorandum incorporating changes from MBI deliberations. OSD then issues each MILDEP its final total obligation authority and manpower controls. The TSOCs we interviewed did not have any input into the staff process and did not advocate at the MBI meeting.

the GCCs (see Appendix A for details). More broadly, staff officers often misunderstand these documents, the degree to which the agreements are authoritative, and their own obligation to abide by them. Most AOs mistakenly believe that these MOAs serve simply as restatements of instructions found in other documents.

In our interviews with USSOCOM headquarters staff, there was resistance to suggestions that the MOAs should be modified to include clearer definitions. Part of this reluctance may stem from the difficulties experienced in coming to agreement on the definitions of *Service-common* and *SOF-peculiar*. The headquarters staff felt that these differences were best settled through other agreements and on a case-by-case basis.

There is limited awareness of the requirements of Pub. L. 112-81, the National Defense Authorization Act for Fiscal Year 2012, particularly Section 904, which calls for the development of MOAs between USSOCOM and the MILDEPs for the establishment of processes and milestones by which numbers and types of enabling capabilities of the general purpose forces can be identified and dedicated to fulfill the training and operational requirements of USSOCOM. Those familiar with the legislation tend to treat it narrowly and literally and do not appreciate its potential to help them to negotiate with the MILDEPs to define funding responsibilities more clearly.

Resolving disputes over funding responsibilities is one of the most difficult tasks confronting TSOC staff officers. DoDD 5100.03 provides only that unresolved disputes be forwarded to the Secretary of Defense for a decision. Short of that, AOs generally attempt to resolve deadlocks through a combination of persuasion and bargaining. They often view the ability to be able to come to an understanding with their peers in the CCSA, the GCC, or MILDEP component command staff as a matter of personal competence. They rarely consult their Staff Judge Advocates (SJAs) on the subject and typically believe they have wide discretion to handle the matter. Their approach often results in lengthy email exchanges and can take months—roughly five months in the CRE example. Table A.1 in Appendix A summarizes key provisions of nine DoD MOAs that could be used as a guide to restructuring the MOAs between USSOCOM and the Services.

The MOAs that USSOCOM has with the Air Force and the Navy incorporate by reference DoDD 5100.3, which has been canceled and superseded by DoDD 5100.03. This is important because DoDD 5100.03 includes new definitions of *administrative and logistical support*, *Combatant Command Support Agent*, *subordinate unified command*, and *Theater Special Operations Command* that were not included in DoDD 5100.3. Additional responsibilities for the combatant commands that were not present in DoDD 5100.3 are enumerated in Enclosure 2 of DoDD 5100.03. Enclosure 3 of DoDD 5100.03 lists and identifies TSOCs as subordinate unified commands, an important change from DoDD 5100.3. Appendix A provides further detail on this issue.

CHAPTER THREE

Conclusions and Recommendations

Making USSOCOM the CCSA for the TSOCs is not a desirable course of action because it is unlikely, on its own, to ensure that the TSOCs can overcome their present funding challenges and because it would expose USSOCOM and DoD to additional, unnecessary expenses associated with tracking, accounting, reporting, and reimbursing Service-common expenses and BOS. However, with the TSOCs now assigned to USSOCOM,[1] CDRUSSOCOM has an opportunity to pursue a course of action that anticipates funding disputes and seeks to either eliminate them or shorten their duration. The recommendations we present in this chapter fall into three categories. The first category pertains to reducing the number and duration of funding disputes; the second seeks to increase USSOCOM's flexibility in funding validated but unfunded requirements; the third pertains to MOAs between the Services and USSOCOM.

Recommendations Pertaining to the Dispute Resolution Process

Recommendations 1 through 4 could be implemented in the near term, while the recommendations concerning funding flexibility may involve changes in the funding process that could require further vetting before action is taken. Each recommendation is consistent with the intent of DoDD 5100.03.

---

[1] The GCCs retain OPCON, i.e., command authority that may be exercised by commanders at any echelon at or below the level of combatant command. OPCON is inherent in combatant command authority and may be delegated within the command. OPCON is the authority to perform those functions of command over subordinate forces involving organizing and employing commands and forces, assigning tasks, designating objectives, and giving authoritative direction necessary to accomplish the mission. OPCON includes authoritative direction over all aspects of military operations and joint training necessary to accomplish missions assigned to the command. OPCON should be exercised through the commanders of subordinate organizations. Normally, this authority is exercised through subordinate joint force commanders and Service and/or functional component commanders. OPCON normally provides full authority to organize commands and forces and to employ those forces as the commander in OPCON considers necessary to accomplish assigned missions; it does not, in and of itself, include authoritative direction for logistics or matters of administration, discipline, internal organization, or unit training (Joint Publication 1-02, 2010).

1. To reduce the opportunities for funding disagreements, USSOCOM should incorporate a financial planning element into the existing Rehearsal of Concept drill. Specifically, USSOCOM should expand the drill and synchronize it with the budget planning process to link potential funding sources, the responsibilities for funding, and the flow of funding to the requirements generated during it. Identifying funding early in the requirements determination process would allow USSOCOM, GCCs, CCSAs, and MILDEP component commands to link operational priorities to the deliberate budget planning process for the year of execution, identify gaps in funding and potential requirements to reprogram funds, and make informed inputs to the POM process. This should also include the identification of mission elements where congressional appropriation language may represent a hurdle to the desired funding. We suggest that the lead for implementation be J-8 or OSD(C).[2]

2. DoDD 5100.03 establishes a high-level dispute resolution process intended to reduce the frequency and duration of funding disputes. At lower levels and consistent with the intent of DoDD 5100.03, USSOCOM and USD(C) should develop approaches to improve the ability of the CCSAs, GCCs, and MILDEP component commands to distinguish between Service-common (MFP-2) and SOF-peculiar (MFP-11) expenses and to resolve disputes expeditiously. Currently, there is no formal lower-level dispute resolution process, and J-5 is primarily responsible for drafting MOAs and other inter-Service agreements. The process employed by J-5 to draft these agreements calls for the involvement of the SJA[3] only at the end of the process in a review capacity. We recommend greater participation and collaboration between J-5 and the SJA earlier in the agreement development process. Specifically,

   • Pub. L. 112-81 § 904, passed in December 2011,[4] requires annual review of MOAs between USSOCOM and the MILDEPs and the establishment of processes and milestones by which numbers and types of enabling capabilities of the general-purpose forces can be identified and dedicated to fulfill the training and operational requirements of USSOCOM. In compliance with this law, USSOCOM should review and modify MOAs[5] between itself and the MILDEPs.

---

[2] J-8 is the Joint Staff Directorate for Force Structure, Resource, and Assessment (Department of Defense, Joint Publication 1-02, 2010).

[3] Staff Judge Advocate—(DOD): A judge advocate so designated in the Army, Air Force, or Marine Corps, and the principal legal advisor of a Navy, Coast Guard, or joint force command who is a judge advocate. Also called SJA. Source: JP 1-04, Joint Publication 1-02, *DOD Dictionary of Military and Associated Terms*, November 8, 2010, as amended through June 15, 2013.

[4] When asked, USSOCOM staff were not generally aware of Pub. L. 112-81. Those who were aware of it tended to apply a narrow, literal definition of the intent of this law and seemed reluctant to explore the possibility of using its provisions to improve definitions and clarify responsibilities for support to USSOCOM.

[5] The December 1, 1989, memorandum from then–Secretary of Defense Donald Atwood to the Secretaries of the Military Departments, the Chairman of the Joint Chiefs of Staff, Under Secretaries of Defense, Assistant

- The revised MOAs should include:

    - Expanded definitions of common terms, including a more specific description of what *Service-common* means to each MILDEP and definitions of *BOS*[6] in the context of SOF requirements. The definitions should be included as an annex to the MOAs between USSOCOM and the Services that details common uses of MFP-2 and MFP-11 funding (see Appendix A).
    - A dispute resolution process that designates a single point of contact (SPOC) for both the MILDEPs and USSOCOM concerning the MOA and MOA annexes and that establishes a series of triggers that will elevate disputes and encourage timely resolution. Annex N of the current USSOCOM–U.S. Army MOA could serve as a model for a dispute resolution process. Appendix A presents a detailed analysis of the existing MOAs and recommended changes. We suggest that the lead for implementation be J-5 with the SJA.

- Provide staff training and reference materials and a DoD-wide coordinated guidebook to assist stakeholders in making preliminary determinations between Service-common expenses, BOS, and SOF-peculiar expenses. All stakeholders, including TSOC AOs, CCSA, GCC, and MILDEP component command comptrollers; financial management officials; and contracting officers, should have access to the content. We suggest that the lead for implementation be J-3.[7]
- Require greater involvement of the SJAs in arriving at determinations of funding responsibilities. Take advantage of SJA channels to reach consensus with both the SJAs of the CCSAs, GCCs, and MILDEP component commands and the applicable fiscal counsel in both the DoD components and OSD on respective funding responsibilities for various USSOCOM activities and initiatives. We suggest that the lead for implementation be J-5 with the SJA.

3. To address the issues associated with financial planning, especially for validated but unfunded USSOCOM initiatives and operations, USSOCOM should

---

Secretaries of Defense, Comptroller, Commander-in-Chief United States Special Operations Command, and the Director of Administration and Management establishes the use of MOAs to delineate responsibilities between the Services and USSOCOM and provides guidance for developing and implementing the SOF program and budget.

[6] BOS provides the resources to operate the bases, installations, camps, posts, and stations of the MILDEPs and the Defense Health Program. These resources sustain mission capability, ensure quality of life, and enhance workforce productivity, and fund personnel and infrastructure support. Personnel support includes food and housing services for unaccompanied and deployed forces; religious services and programs; payroll support; personnel management; and morale, welfare, and recreation services to military members and their families. Infrastructure support includes utility system operations; installation equipment maintenance; engineering services, including fire protection, crash rescue, custodial services, refuse collection, snow removal, and lease of real property; security protection and law enforcement; and transportation motor pool operations (Office of the Under Secretary of Defense [Comptroller], undated).

[7] J-3 is the operations directorate of a joint staff (Department of Defense, Joint Publication 1-02, 2010).

- Establish J-8 as the center of expertise at USSOCOM HQ responsible for shep-herding the TSOCs through the requirements determination and funding pro-cess. The alignment of the TSOCs under USSOCOM provides an opportunity to greatly improve information sharing across the TSOCs and to leverage the financial expertise at the HQ level. This centralized funding center should be expert in the multiple funding sources, should oversee the TSOCs' requirements determination process to ensure the applicability of funding, and should draft DEPORDs and EXORDs with the required level of specificity to reduce ambigu-ity with regard to the funding source. We suggest that the lead for implementa-tion be J-8.

4. Establish a collaborative annual training program for the MILDEPs, TSOCs, SJAs, and USSOCOM HQ staff to inform all parties involved in funding decisions of their roles and responsibilities, the dispute resolution process, and details of the MOAs and possible issues introduced by new legislation or regulation. This would help reduce the tendency of trying to reach local agreement on the basis of personal relationships. We suggest that the lead for implementation be J-3.

All of the above recommendations require a USSOCOM HQ center of exper-tise to manage funding, budgeting, and execution, as well as the implementation of a dispute resolution structure and clearer definitions of MFP-2 and MFP-11 in the MOAs. They are offered with a clear understanding of the pressures to reduce defense component manning; the current environment exerts an even more taxing burden on resource application.

Recommendations Pertaining to Funding Flexibility

The unpredictable, often time-sensitive nature of USSOCOM's funding demands on the MILDEPs will continue to be a source of dispute and delay under current resource allocation processes. The burden placed by unfunded requirements on the MILDEPs is likely to increase with the projected reductions in funding for other contingency operations (e.g., OCO).

If the President and Congress want to promote a more flexible and responsive employment of SOF by the GCCs, this will require improvement in the way the TSOCs arrange funding of validated unfunded operations.[8] There are several existing funding mechanisms designed to provide funding flexibility in the face of uncertain requirements. Three of these funding options could serve as models to better manage

---

[8]   Under GSN, SOF could increasingly be the tool of choice for more missions, and they would be geographi-cally positioned to carry out more missions, which implies their increased use. If the President and Congress move forward with an expanded use of SOF as implied under the GSN, increased funding flexibility would allow for more effective and efficient employment of these capabilities.

the funding of validated unfunded requirements while maintaining accountability and ensuring that funds are used for the purpose intended by Congress. Any of the options would enable DoD to provide USSOCOM with the flexibility to react quickly to emergent demands, while providing the MILDEPs the time to build the unforeseen requirement into the POM. None of these options is currently being used to augment funding appropriated by Congress for this specific purpose. They are concepts at this point; how they would operate, if pursued, would have to be detailed along with assessing the implications for potential base-budget transfers.

All three options require a USSOCOM HQ center of expertise to manage funding, budgeting, and execution, as well as the implementation of a dispute resolution structure and clearer definitions of MFP-2 and MFP-11 in the MOAs. The scope of this research limited further exploration of these options, including challenges to implementation. However, we recommend that USSOCOM and the MILDEPs pursue with USD(C) one of these options or develop others.[9]

Option A. Request that OSD work with Congress to authorize a SOF support Central Transfer Account (CTA) that would take the form of a single line-item appropriation similar to the counternarcotics CTA (PBD 678, 1989) and would constitute a reserve to fund unanticipated requirements during execution. The SOF support CTA would be managed by ASD SO/LIC to provide funding for unfunded SOF support requirements. The MILDEPs, GCCs, and MILDEP component commands would request allocations from ASD SOL/IC working through USD(C) and draw upon the fund to support SOF initiatives in their respective AORs. The CTA would have no effect on regularly budgeted Service-common and BOS expenses. As with the counternarcotics CTA, the OSD Inspector General would conduct annual audits. The Services and other consumers of CTA funding would use their internal financial management systems to track funding activities.

Option B. USSOCOM could request authority from OSD to use MFP-11 to fund all validated requirements for emergent operations during their initial start-up phase, with the understanding that continuing funding responsibility would be the subject of MILDEP deliberations during the normal resource allocation process. USSOCOM would provide a detailed accounting that would allow for the identification of requirements that should have been funded using MFP-2. This would inform annual account

---

[9] For example, some type of revolving account might be established to anticipate unfunded requirements for SOF. Although no such mechanism is currently in place, some type of revolving account could be established by law. This would require defining and documenting the SOF requirements that would be covered, establishing a cost structure, and exploring the legal ramifications and potential regulatory and legislative changes that would be required. It is beyond the scope of this research to explore the details of a revolving fund; however, such a fund could provide a solution to the underlying issue of funding flexibility identified in this report.

reconciliation between USSOCOM and the MILDEPs if functional transfers were deemed necessary.

Option C. The third option would be for the MILDEPS to establish a flexible operating account using existing O&M funds to anticipate emergent SOF support funding requirements. The MILDEPs have some flexibility to make "fact of life" adjustments to the baseline budget. A forecast of SOF funding requirements, along with the GCCs' priorities, could establish the baseline flexible operating account. Funds to support this account could be administered by the MILDEPs based on the GCCs' priorities and in accordance with the regulations governing transfers within O&M accounts.

Any of these options would enable DoD to have flexible SOF to react quickly to emergency demands, while providing the time to build unforeseen requirements into their POMs and budget or, if necessary, seek supplemental funding. All options require a USSOCOM HQ center of expertise to manage the funding, budgeting, and execution, as well as the implementation of a dispute resolution structure and clearer definitions of MFP-2 and MFP-11 in the MOAs.

Recommendations Pertaining to Memoranda of Agreement

Appendix A discusses the rationale for the recommendations presented below. These recommendations are directed at reducing USSOCOM staff churn and potential causes of disputes between USSOCOM and the MILDEPs concerning MFP-2 and MFP-11 funding. Implementing these recommendations could resolve many of the problems currently experienced by the TSOCs. Currently, the MOAs that USSOCOM has with the MILDEPs are idle, providing little utility. They can and should be leveraged to obtain the level of support that USSOCOM's operations require. Pub. L. 112-81, § 904, provides USSOCOM with the authority to update these MOAs annually and to require greater detail in them. Turning USSOCOM's MOAs with the MILDEPs into useful tools requires that they be updated in four key ways:

1. **Include detailed descriptions of what *Service-common* means to each MILDEP.** Include a mutually agreed decision tree similar to the example in Figure 3.1. Currently, the standard definition in DoDD 5100.03 (or its predecessor, 5100.3), which is referenced as the definition of *Service-common* in USSOCOM's MOAs, states that "items and services defined as Service-common by one Military Service are not necessarily Service-common for all other Military Services." This is a loophole that permits a representative to argue that what USSOCOM wants and needs is not Service-common for his or her particular MILDEP. This loophole must be closed. So many MFP-2 funding decisions are tied to the definition of *Service-common* that a more comprehensive and detailed definition of what the term means to the Army, the Navy, and

Figure 3.1
Example Decision Tree

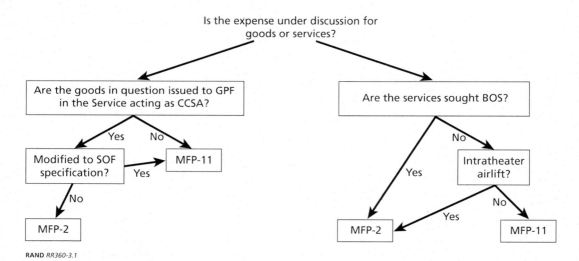

RAND *RR360-3.1*

the Air Force in conjunction with programs, systems, equipment, materiel, supplies, and services would clarify the task of USSOCOM staff and reduce staff churn, as well as reduce or abbreviate disputes with the MILDEPs.

2. **Include a dispute resolution process in each MILDEP MOA.** A clearly designated process for resolving disputes at levels lower than the Commander, Special Operations Command and the Administrative Assistant to Secretary of the Air Force (for example) is required to expeditiously resolve disputes between the parties, particularly concerning the use of MFP-2 and MFP-11 funding for USSOCOM operations. Annex N to the Army MOA with USSOCOM provides a useful model for a dispute resolution process.

3. **Include definitions (or better definitions) of BOS, MFP-2, and MFP-11.** The Air Force MOA does not contain a definition of Base Operating Support. The Army's MOA with USSOCOM, Annex E, "Administrative, Logistics and Installation Base Support Services," pp. 3–5, provides specific details about the baseline level of Service-common support to Army SOF. These details concerning Base Operating Support appear to be specific and comprehensive and could serve as a useful model for MOAs that USSOCOM has with the Navy and the Air Force.

4. **Include a Single Point of Contact (SPOC) for each MOA and its individual annexes, appendixes, and enclosures.** SPOCs who serve as subject-matter experts on the provisions of the MOA annexes could reduce staff churn and disputes with the MILDEPs concerning interpretation of the annexes. The chal-

lenge would then be to empower the SPOCs as spokespersons for the MILDEPs and USSOCOM.

The addition of a dispute resolution process annex, or a SPOC, or a definition of *BOS* should be a relatively easy task for USSOCOM's J-5 staff and SJA. However, defining what *Service-common* means for each of the MILDEPs probably will require the services of a neutral third party. Currently, experts on both sides of the Service-common issue are entrenched in their positions, and it is unlikely that USSOCOM and each MILDEP will be able to expeditiously negotiate a definition. Therefore, a neutral third party—perhaps OSD(C)—could meet with the MILDEPs and with USSOCOM and review available appropriation cognizance precedents to develop a robust definition of *Service-common* for use by the parties in their MOAs and in their dealings with each other. The GSN is projected to increase the number of SOF deployments and overseas basing, especially to austere locations, and fewer OCO dollars will be available. The prospect of more frequent, validated but often unfunded deployments and reduced funding flexibility makes it necessary for USSOCOM to develop robust processes to support funding for emerging initiatives and to reduce the time lost by USSOCOM over funding disputes.

Memoranda of Agreement

Introduction

This appendix provides a general definition of MOAs and their functions, along with a review and critique of three of the MOAs between USSOCOM the MILDEPs. It offers examples of other MOAs between DoD and other U.S. government entities, highlighting the positive attributes that we recommend for inclusion in USSOCOM's MOAs. Specific recommendations are presented for refining the USSOCOM MOAs.

Background

An MOA is used in commercial as well as military settings to document an agreement between the parties. Specifically, an MOA serves as an instrument to regulate and manage the relationship of the parties in the performance of their agreement.

USSOCOM Directive 1-7, February 9, 2012, defines an MOA as

> a document that defines general areas of responsibility and conditional agreement between two or more Parties, normally headquarters or major command level components. The actions of one Party within the agreement are dependent upon the actions of another Party (e.g., one party agrees to provide support if the other Party provides materials). *MOAs (that) establish responsibilities for providing recurring reimbursable support should be supplemented with support agreements that define the support, basis for reimbursement for each category of support, the billing and payment process, and other terms and conditions of the agreement* (emphasis added).

Structure of DoD MOAs

The structure of a DoD MOA is determined by the needs of the parties and their particular agreement. Generally, an MOA will include the subject, the parties, references or authorities for the responsibilities outlined in the agreement, the purpose of the agreement, the background of the agreement (outlining pertinent history of the agreement), consistent with current or updated joint publications and DoD doctrine relating to the agreement, the responsibilities of each party, a governance provision that describes a dispute resolution process for the parties to the agreement (including a Single Point of Contact, with office and/or job title), the effective date of the agreement, provisions for review and changes to the MOA, the capability to update requirements specific to the parties, and termination provisions. The MOA is signed by the parties to the agreement. Specific details concerning an undertaking by the parties, such as particular arrangements for reimbursable support, a billing and payment process, or a process to be used in case of a specific emergency, are usually included in separate documents that are attached to the MOA, called annexes or appendixes. The annexes follow the structure outlined above and are also signed by the parties and incorporated into the MOA. If important terms related to an annex have not been defined in the cover MOA, they are defined in the annex. If a dispute resolution process has not been defined in the cover MOA, it may be defined in an annex. A SPOC or key person for each side of the agreement is usually designated to expedite clarification of responsibilities and dispute resolution, both in the cover MOA and in each annex.

Authority for USSOCOM MOAs with the MILDEPs

The Deputy Secretary of Defense Memorandum, Guidance for Developing and Implementing Special Forces Program and Budget, 1 December 1989, known as the Atwood Memo, provides that "the attached guidance will serve as the basis for preparing POM- and budget-related Memoranda of Agreement (MOAs) that are necessary to delineate responsibilities between USCINCSOC and the Military Departments." On December 31, 2011, Congress passed Pub. L. 112-81, the National Defense Authorization Act for Fiscal Year 2012. Section 904 of the Act requires annual review of MOAs between USSOCOM and the MILDEPs and "the establishment of processes and milestones by which numbers and types of enabling capabilities of the general purpose forces of the Armed Forces under the jurisdiction of each such Secretary can be identified and dedicated to fulfill the training and operational requirements of special operations forces under the United States Special Operations Command." The law provides that this can be done as an annex to an existing MOA or in a new MOA. It provides leverage for USSOCOM to create MOAs that are more detailed and have increased utility, because they are to be updated annually, rather than every five years, as was previously the case.[1]

---

[1]   The conference report on the bill (p. 679) states, "Memoranda of agreement on identification and dedication of enabling capabilities of general purposed forces to fulfill certain requirements of special operations forces (§ 904)."

The Senate amendment contained a provision (§ 903) that would require each secretary of a MILDEP to enter into an MOA with CDRUSSOCOM establishing the procedures by which the availability of the enabling capabilities of the general purpose forces will be synchronized with the training and deployment cycle of SOF.

Review of USSOCOM MOAs with the MILDEPs

Omissions in the MOAs that USSOCOM has with the MILDEPs can create disputes and problems that ultimately can impact USSOCOM's ability to support the GCCs. The following review highlights omissions in four key areas: (1) defining funding support responsibilities; (2) providing an end-to-end dispute resolution process; (3) providing detailed definitions of Service-common Major Force Program 2 (MFP-2) and SOF-peculiar Major Force Program 11 (MFP-11) funding and BOS; and (4) providing a SPOC to clarify and interpret the MOA and annexes.

USSOCOM MOA with the Department of the Air Force

Funding Provisions. Annex F, "Responsibilities for Planning, Programming, Budgeting and Execution," in Section I, General, subsection b, states that "References 1a, 1g, and 1h [DoDD 5100.3] document functions and responsibilities of Military Departments for support of special operations forces." *Reference 1h, D0DD 5100.3 has been canceled* and superseded by DoDD 5100.03, which contains new and different language that clarifies command relationships and makes explicit the headquarters and BOS responsibilities of a combatant command for its TSOC. This is important because Annex F, Section I (2)(b) provides that "the Department of the AF [Air Force] will program sufficient non-MFP-11 funds to ensure a level of BOS, to include all common-user communications equipment and services required to support AFSOF units on all USAF installation. This BOS support will be *in accordance with reference 1h* and on a non-reimbursable basis. The level of support will be commensurate with other USAF activities. The AF will be responsible for providing Service-common and BOS support to AFSOF whether on AF-owned installations or other Service's installations." *BOS is not defined in either Enclosure 2 of the MOA, "Terms, Definitions and Abbreviations," or Annex F.* Service-common is defined in Enclosure 2 as "Equipment, material, supplies and services adopted by a Military Service for use by its own forces and activities. These include standard military items, base operating support, and the supplies and services provided by a Military Service to support and sustain its own forces, including those assigned to the combatant commands. Items and services defined as Service-common by one Military Service are not necessarily Service-common for all other Military Services." This definition does not clarify what items and services are considered Service-common by the Air Force. Thus, neither Service-common nor BOS has been clearly defined concerning what support the Department of the Air Force must provide USSOCOM on Air Force–owned installations or those of another MILDEP where the Air Force is the CCSA. This creates a basis for disputes between USSOCOM (especially the TSOCs) and the Air Force.

The House bill contained no similar provision. The House receded with a clarifying amendment. The conference report is meant to clarify the bill language. It does not constrain USSOCOM from interpreting the bill as requiring annual and more detailed updates of the MOAs it has with the MILDEPs.

Dispute Resolution Process. The dispute resolution language that appears in the MOA is in the "Overarching MOA Between the U.S. Air Force and USSOCOM," Section 5, Responsibilities, subsection (b). It states that "the Parties jointly resolve any disagreement concerning this MOA. CDRUSSOCOM delegates to the Commander, Air Force Special Operations Command authority to resolve any such disagreements. The SECAF [Secretary of the Air Force] delegates such authority to the Assistant Vice Chief of Staff of the Air Force (AF/CVA). Any matter that cannot be resolved by the above designees shall be presented in writing to the USSOCOM Chief of Staff, the Secretary of the Air Force Administrative Assistant (SAF/AA) for resolution by the signatories." This language does not set out a dispute resolution escalation chain, by office, beginning with AOs. A clearly designated process for resolving disputes at levels lower than CDRUSSOCOM and the SAF/AA is required to expeditiously resolve disputes between the parties, particularly concerning the use of MFP-2 and MFP-11 funding for USSOCOM operations.

Detailed Definitions of MFP-2, MFP-11, and BOS Funding. Enclosure 2 of the "Overarching MOA Between the U.S. Air Force and USSOCOM," which addresses "Terms, Definitions and Abbreviations," uses a three-sentence definition of *Service-common* that does not address what specific items and services are considered Service-common by the Department of the Air Force. The definition in the MOA states that "items and services defined as Service-common by one Military Service are not necessarily Service-common for all other Military Services." Failure to include a detailed, Department of the Air Force–specific definition of what it considers Service-common is likely to create uncertainty on the part of USSOCOM staff and generate protracted disputes between USSOCOM and the MILDEP. BOS is not defined in either Enclosure 2 of the MOA, "Terms, Definitions and Abbreviations," or in Annex F, "Responsibilities for Planning, Programming, Budgeting and Execution." In Annex F, Section II, (2), "Planning and Programming," subsection (c)(h) provides that the Department of the Air Force will provide "Service-common logistics support." Without any definition of *Service-common*, this brief phrase could be subject to many interpretations by both USSOCOM and Department of the Air Force staff. Similarly, Section II, (3), "Budgeting and Execution," subsection (b)(1)(d), provides that "the Department of the Air Force will budget and execute all non-MFP-11 resources in support of AFSOF, including Operations and Maintenance, USAF (O&M), Operations Maintenance, USAF Reserve (O&M) for: Base Operations Support." The absence in the MOA of Department of the Air Force–specific descriptions of what constitutes BOS is likely to create recurring issues for USSOCOM staff, as well as protracted disputes with the Department of the Air Force. Such disputes can delay funding and have a negative impact on USSOCOM's operations.

Single Point of Contact. Only one annex to the Air Force MOA identifies a "proponent" for each of the parties to the agreement. Annex G, "Department of the Air Force

Support to USSOCOM Sensitive Activities/Programs (U)," provides in Section 6 (c) that, "(U) The USSOCOM proponent for this Annex is the Director, Command Operations Review Board. The Department of the Air Force proponent is the SAF/AAZ. Proponents for specific programs or topics are listed in the program-specific Enclosures." A SPOC generally serves as the expert on the subject matter of an agreement like an annex and can address questions about its provisions. The official who executes the document (such as the Administrative Assistant to the Secretary of the Air Force) is not a SPOC. If USSOCOM and the Department of the Air Force agreed to a "proponent" for each party to the MOA in Annex G, there should be no objection to appointing "proponents" or SPOCs for the other annexes. Section 6(c) of Annex G apparently recognizes the need for additional program-specific subject-matter experts, stating that "proponents for specific programs or topics are listed in the program-specific Enclosures." Proponents or SPOCs who serve as subject-matter experts concerning the provisions of the MOA annexes can reduce staff churn and disputes with the Department of the Air Force concerning interpretation of the annexes.

USSOCOM MOA with the Department of the Navy

Funding Provisions. Annex A to Appendix 1, "Responsibilities for Planning, Programming, Budgeting and Execution," in Section 1, General, 1(b) states that "References 1a, 1g, and 1h document functions and responsibilities of military departments for support of special operations forces." As noted previously, *Reference 1h, DoDD 5100.3, has been canceled and superseded by DoDD 5100.03*, which contains new and different language that clarifies command relationships and makes explicit the headquarters and BOS responsibilities of a combatant command for its TSOC. This is important because Annex A to Appendix 1, Subsection 1(d) of Section 1 states, "Programs funded in the appropriations of the DON [Department of the Navy] (Common Service Support), not identified as MFP-11, will consist of programs that support other users in addition to SOF. This includes programs and services funded by Defense Agencies (non-MFP-11) tasked with providing common services to the United States Navy (USN) and United States Marine Corps (USMC). For services or programs (including Quality of Life Programs/Services), define 'common' as any service or program provided to non-SF units or service members. Services shall be made available to Maritime SOF at a rate not less than that provided to other Naval units." It is unlikely that USSOCOM staff, particularly in the TSOCs, will be aware of what services and programs are provided to non-SOF units or service members. Thus, this definition of *Service-common* is likely to lead to guesswork on the part of USSOCOM staff and disputes with the Department of the Navy (DON) over funding support. In Section 1, part 2, "Responsibilities," subsection (b) states that "DON will program sufficient non-MFP-11 funds to ensure a level of BOS, to include all common-user communications equipment and services required to support maritime SOF units on a Navy installation. This BOS support will be in accordance with reference 1k and on a nonreimbursable basis. The level of support will be commensurate with other USN and/or USMC activities." DoD Instruction 4000.19, 9 August 1995, provides only general categories of intergovernmental or interagency support, most of which have nothing to do with base operations. Thus, neither Service-common nor BOS has been clearly defined in terms of what support DON must provide USSOCOM on Navy-owned installations or those of another MILDEP and creates a basis for disputes between USSOCOM (especially the TSOCs) and DON.

Dispute Resolution Process. The "Overarching Memorandum of Agreement" and the annexes, appendixes, and enclosures do not contain a dispute resolution process.

Detailed Definitions of MFP-2, MFP-11, and BOS Funding. Enclosure 2 of the "Overarching MOA Between Department of the Navy and USSOCOM," which concerns "Terms, Definitions and Abbreviations," uses a three-sentence definition of *Service-common* that does not address what specific items and services are considered Service-common by the Department of the Navy. The definition in the MOA states that "items and services defined as Service-common by one Military Service are not necessarily Service-common for all other Military Services." Failure to include a detailed Department of the Navy–specific definition of what is meant by Service-common is likely to create uncertainty on the part of USSOCOM staff and generate protracted disputes between USSOCOM and the MILDEP. Enclosure 2 states in 2(e) that "for the purposes of this MOA, BOS will be defined as the common base support categories listed in DoD Instruction 4000.19, 9 August 1995," which provides only general categories of intergovernmental or interagency support, most of which have nothing to do with base operations. It is notable that the rest of Section 2(e) states that "the category definitions should be modified and expanded for each agreement to clearly define the specific support that will be provided in each category. Additional support categories may be developed to define services not included in reference publication."

Single Point of Contact. No SPOCs or proponents are included in the overarching MOA with the Department of the Navy or its annexes, appendixes, and enclosures.

USSOCOM MOA with the Department of the Army
Funding Provisions. Annex F to the "Overarching Memorandum of Agreement Between Department of the Army and USSOCOM" provides a level of detail for planning and programming that is not present in the MOAs with the Department of the Air Force or the Department of the Navy. The annex correctly cites DoDD 5100.03, 9 February 2011, in the references section, and it attempts to define *Service-common* in greater detail than the standard definition provided in DoDD 5100.03. Annex F, Section I, 1(g) states that, "the term 'Service-common,' when used in this annex in conjunction with programs, systems, equipment, materiel, supplies, and services, refers

to those elements common throughout the Department of the Army that are classified standard in accordance with SB700-20, Cataloging of Supplies and Equipment, Army Adopted Items of Materials and List of Reportable Items. Service-common is defined in reference 1p (Joint Publication 1-02, Department of Defense Dictionary of Military and Associated Terms, 31 December 2010[2]) and Enclosure 2 of the Overarching DA-USSOCOM MOA.)" The definitions of *Service-common* and *base operations* (BASOPS) are critical to interpreting the specific responsibilities of the Department of the Army for providing non–MFP-11 support to USSOCOM. Annex F, Section I, Subsection 2(b), "Responsibilities," states that "Department of the Army will: (1) Program sufficient non-MFP-11 funds to ensure an appropriate level of Service-common and BASOPS, to include all common-user communications equipment and services required to support ARSOF [Army Special Operations Forces] units. This BASOPS support will be in accordance with reference 1h and on a non-reimbursable basis. The level of Service-common and BASOPS support will be commensurate with that of other Department of the Army units and activities. The Department of the Army will be responsible for providing or facilitating Service-common and BASOPS support to ARSOF whether on MILDEP-owned installations or other Service's installations." There are problems with this statement. First, reference 1h is Department of Defense Instruction 4000.19, "Interservice and Intergovernmental Support," 9 August 1995, which sets out broadly defined categories of intergovernmental and inter-Service support, most of which have nothing to do with BOS. Second, given the unique and specialized mission of the GSN, it is likely that the requirements of USSOCOM will be different from, not commensurate with, "that of other Army units and activities." If the Department of the Army's requirement for Service-common and BOS to ARSOF is that they be commensurate with or equivalent to those "of Army units and activities," then there are likely to be disputes over programming adequate non–MFP-11 funds.

Dispute Resolution Process. The "Overarching Memorandum of Agreement" between the Department of the Army and USSOCOM, Section 5, "Responsibilities," provides two sentences concerning dispute resolution: "Commander, USASOC and Commander, JSOC are authorized direct liaison by the CDRUSSOCOM to discuss any concerns and receive any disagreements arising under this MOA with the Vice Chief of Staff of the Army. For those issues that cannot be resolved at that level, written notice will be provided to the USSOCOM Chief of Staff and the Administrative Assistant to the Secretary of the Army, and referred to the CDRUSSOCOM and the Secretary of the Army, respectively, for resolution." This language does not set out a dispute

---

[2] "Equipment, material, supplies, and services adopted by a Military Service for use by its own forces and activities. These include standard military items, base operating support, and the supplies and services provided by a Military Service to support and sustain its own forces, including those assigned to the combatant commands. Items and services defined as Service-common by one Military Service are not necessarily Service-common for all other Military Services" (Department of Defense, Joint Publication 1-02, 2010).

resolution escalation chain, by office, beginning with AOs. A clearly designated process for resolving disputes at levels lower than CDRUSSOCOM and the Vice Chief of Staff of the Army is required to expeditiously resolve disputes between the parties, particularly concerning the use of MFP-2 and MFP-11 funding for USSOCOM operations.

Detailed Definitions of MFP-2, MFP-11, and BOS Funding. The Department of the Army MOA with USSOCOM includes an attempt in Annex F to provide a definition of *Service-common* that is more robust and useful than the standard military dictionary definition. However, so many MFP-2 funding decisions are tied to the definition of *Service-common* that a more comprehensive and detailed Department of the Army–specific definition of *Service-common* in conjunction with programs, systems, equipment, materiel, supplies, and services would clarify the task for USSOCOM staff and reduce staff churn, as well as reduce or abbreviate disputes with the Army. In Annex E, "Administrative, Logistics and Installation Base Support Services," pp. 3–5 define and provide specific details about the baseline level of common Service support to ARSOF. These details concerning BOS appear to be specific and comprehensive and could serve as a useful model for MOAs that USSOCOM has with the Department of the Navy and the Department of the Air Force.

Single Point of Contact. No SPOCs are identified for either party in the overarching MOA or its annexes, appendixes, or enclosures.

Good Models for USSOCOM MOAs

Annex N to the MOA between the Department of the Army and USSOCOM provides a good model for a dispute resolution process. The annex formally establishes the United States Army–United States Special Operations Command Board (ASB) as an intragovernmental committee. The mission of the ASB is to address bilateral issues of concern, which may include (but are not limited to) doctrine, concepts, capabilities, requirements, and programs. The ASB receives its direction from the Chief of Staff of the Army and CDRUSSOCOM. It will report recommendations, as endorsed by its General Officer Steering Committee, to the CSA and CDRUSSOCOM. The ASB permanently comprises two bodies: the Committee and the Council of Colonels. Other subject-matter expert teams may be created in support of the ASB to study specific issues; however, such teams will serve only in an advisory capacity to the ASB. The annex describes in detail a process for issue identification, issue development, issue review, and issue resolution. This type of process could be adapted easily for resolution of disputes between the Department of the Army and USSOCOM concerning other annexes of the MOA. It could also serve as a model for a dispute resolution annex for MOAs between the USSOCOM and the Departments of the Navy and the Air Force.

Another useful model is the Support Agreement between the Commander in Chief United States European Command (USEUCOM) and the Commander in Chief United States Army, Europe (USAREUR) and Seventh Army. The purpose of this agreement is to "establish and delineate responsibilities for the provision of administrative and logistics support by HQ USAREUR to HQ USEUCOM, Patch Barracks, the Vaihingen Military Subcommunity (VMSC), and HQ USEUCOM elements at the Stuttgart Army Airfield (SAAF)." The agreement has a 25-page annex that includes a detailed delineation of support requirements that could serve as a useful model for USSOCOM MOA annexes. The agreement also contains a definitions section and a detailed discussion of funding sources, as well as the appointment of a SPOC.

The MOA between DoD and the Department of State on U.S. government Private Security Contractors (PSCs) is intended to "clearly define the authority and responsibility for the accountability and operations of USG Private Security Contractors (PSCs) in Iraq." Section V of the MOA addresses "Implementation, Coordination and Dispute Resolution." Subsection B of Section V sets out requirements for meeting quarterly, or more frequently, concerning the implementation of the MOA by the parties, and the escalation path, on either side of the agreement, for issues or disputes requiring resolution. Annex A, "Deliverables," includes both a definitions section and a policy/definitions section. Section VII sets out a detailed procedure for how the Multi-National Force–Iraq (MNF-I) and the U.S. Embassy will closely coordinate the immediate response to any serious incident involving a U.S. government PSC.

Table A.1 summarizes key provisions of nine DoD MOAs that provide useful models for USSOCOM. It shows which MOAs contain detailed definitions sections, detailed discussions of funding sources, dispute resolution processes, and appointment of a SPOC.

Table A.1
Review of Existing MOAs

	Detailed Definitions Section	Detailed Discussion of Funding Sources	Dispute Resolution	Appointment of Single Point of Contact
MOA between the Department of Commerce and DoD regarding interagency operation of weather surveillance radar (2008)	Yes	Yes	Yes	Yes
MOA between DoD and the Department of State on private security contractors (2007)	Yes	No	Yes	Yes
Support Agreement between USEUCOM and USAREUR (1988)	Yes	Yes	No	Yes
Sample MOA between USAESCH and customer (2005)	No	Yes	Yes	Yes
MOA between MDA and United States Army Acquisition Support Center (2008)	No	Yes	Yes[a]	Yes
MOA between DoD and the Department of Energy (2010)	No	Yes	No	Yes
MOA between the DoD Missile Defense Agency and NASA (2003)	No	Yes	No	Yes
MOA between USSOCOM and U.S. Immigration and Customs Enforcement (2012)	No	Yes	No	Yes
MOA between the Department of Veterans Affairs and DoD for processing payments for disability compensation (2010)	No	Yes	No	No

[a] Not detailed.

Funding Sources

This appendix discusses some of the important funding sources that are or have been available for USSOCOM's operations. It provides an overview of the Defense Program and Major Force Programs 2 and 11 (MFP-2 and MFP-11), then the subsequent sections describe a type of funding, the source of the funds, and the limitations on their use. In a few instances, a description of the purpose of the funds is provided. Each section also summarizes the provisions of the legislation and provides the text of the actual legislation.

1. Overview of the Future Years Defense Program and Major Force Programs 2 and 11

A. Introduction

The Office of the Secretary of Defense (OSD) develops the Future Years Defense Program (FYDP), the official document that summarizes forces and resources associated with programs approved by the Secretary of Defense (prescribed in Program Decision Memoranda (PDMs), Program Change Decisions (PCDs), budget decisions, and other Secretary of Defense decision documents) for DoD. It reflects the total resources programmed by DoD by fiscal year.[1]

The FYDP is composed of 11 major force programs (six combat force–oriented programs and five support programs) used as a basis for internal DoD program appropriations. Hence, it serves a purpose of cross-walking the internal review structure between major force programs, appropriations, and the Services and defense agencies, which is output-oriented with the congressional review structure, which is input-oriented.

This three-dimensional structure, illustrated in Figure B.1, and attendant review process provide a comprehensive approach to accounting for, estimating, identifying, and allocating resources to individual or logical groups or organizational entities, and major combat force or support programs referred to as program elements.

---

[1] DFAS-IN Manual 37-100-12, *The Army Management Structure General Information OSD Program Component (FY2012-Change 3)*, August 31, 2011, at 14-OSDPG-1 to 14-OSDPG-3.

Figure B.1
Future Years Defense Program Structure

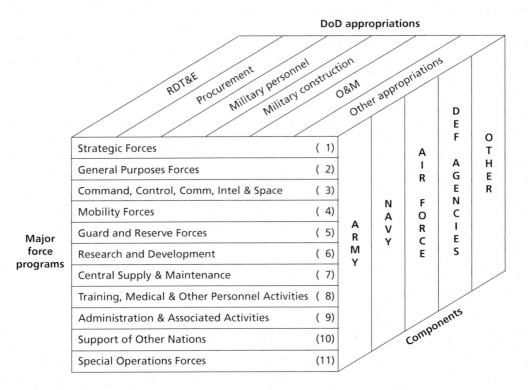

SOURCE: Defense Acquisition University, undated.
RAND *RR360-B.1*

Such a program element describes the force unit, financial, and manpower data, including support requirements organic to the unit, associated with a division, brigade, company, ship, aircraft squadron, and centralized supporting activity not organic to the unit, such as a supply and maintenance depot, recruiting and training activity, individual and professional training, and health and medical facility.[2]

Currently, the following resource identification processes for FYDP data are used:[3]

"a. Research, Development, Test, and Evaluation (RDT&E). R&D project costs normally aggregate directly into program elements; however, certain overhead costs may be spread across all projects when they cannot be related directly to a specific project, or accumulated in management and support program elements.

---

[2] DFAS-IN Manual 37-100-12, The Army Management Structure General Information OSD Program Component (FY2012-Change 3), August 31, 2011 at 14-OSDPG-1 to 14-OSDPG-3.

[3] DFAS-IN Manual 37-100-12, The Army Management Structure General Information OSD Program Component (FY2012-Change 3), August 31, 2011 at 14-OSDPG-1 to 14-OSDPG-3.

"b. Procurement. Procurement dollars are identified to program elements by one of the following:

"(1) Procurement line items representing major weapon systems are directly associated with the appropriate program element or elements in accordance with the mission or missions assigned to the weapon system; unit-related items are associated with program elements according to algorithms that identify units, their relative wartime deployment priority, the equipment authorizations for each unit, the worldwide asset position for equipment items, projected loss rates and the Authorized Acquisition Objective (AAO) for those items; and a mathematical distribution is made to the program element based on these factors.

"(2) Some items are based on historical distribution of identical or similar items being replaced.

"(3) Some support resources, such as automobiles and some utility aircraft, are allocated to base operations program elements in accordance with type and size of mission being supported.

"c. Military Construction. When a construction project is identified, the FYDP major program of the dominant user is determined. As the project moves through the review and approval process, a specific program element is determined and assigned.

"d. Operation and Maintenance. Several methods are used to identify operation and maintenance costs to program elements.

"(1) Force-related resources are applied according to workload requirements (such as flying or steaming hours or overhaul schedules) of force units within each program element.

"(2) Operation and maintenance for reserve components are assigned to those known requirements in specific program elements and the balance is applied according to manpower and strengths.

"(3) Supply and maintenance resources are usually identified according to a number of workload measures and programmed equipment utilization rates.

"(4) Training resources in Program 8 are based on training load requirements for projected mission needs. Unit training resources of the major mission programs are identified by force requirements.

"(5) Medical resource requirements are based on a medical workload factor.

"e. Military Personnel Dollars. Military personnel costs are applied to program elements by a computation of average salaries times the number of personnel for each program element.

"f. Manpower

"(1) Military

"(a) End strengths are normally aggregated directly into program elements based on the program element identification of each unit.

"(b) Unstructured spaces (trainees, transients, patients, prisoners, and students) are computed based on anticipated gains and losses and authorizations for units in all FYDP programs.

"(2) Civilian. Civilian manpower is aggregated directly into program elements based on unit/program element relationships."

B. Major Force Programs

A program is an aggregation of program elements that reflects a force mission or a support mission of DoD and contains the resources needed to achieve an objective or plan. It reflects fiscal year time-phasing of mission objectives to be accomplished and the means proposed for their accomplishment.[4]

The FYDP includes 11 major force programs, including MFP-2 (General Purpose Forces) and MFP-11 (Special Operations Forces). The major programs of the FYDP fall within the general organizational areas of responsibility within the Office of the Secretary of Defense. However, because resources in these programs may overlap areas of management and functional responsibility, the programs are not considered to be the exclusive responsibility of any one particular organizational element of the Office of the Secretary of Defense.[5]

In summary, a major force program reflects a macro-level force mission or a support mission of DoD and contains the resources necessary to achieve a broad objective or plan. It reflects fiscal year time-phasing of mission objectives and the means proposed for their accomplishment.

C. Creation of Major Force Program 11—Special Operations Forces

In FY 1987, Pub. L. 99-661 created a major force program element for SOF.[6] The statute in question currently provides the following:

Text of the statute:[7]
"(f) Budget. In addition to the activities of a combatant command for which funding may be requested under section 166(b) of this title [10 U.S.C. § 166(b)], the budget proposal of the special operations command shall include requests for funding for—

---

[4]   DFAS-IN Manual 37-100-12, The Army Management Structure General Information OSD Program Component (FY2012-Change 3), August 31, 2011 at 14-OSDPG-1 to 14-OSDPG-3.

[5]   DFAS-IN Manual 37-100-12, The Army Management Structure General Information OSD Program Component (FY2012-Change 3), August 31, 2011 at 14-OSDPG-1 to 14-OSDPG-3.

[6]   Major force program category; budget; commanders. Act Nov. 14, 1986, Pub. L. 99-661, Div A, Title XIII, Part B, § 1311, 100 Stat. 3985.

[7]   10 U.S.C. § 167 (2013).

"(1) development and acquisition of special operations–peculiar equipment; and

"(2) acquisition of other material, supplies, or services that are peculiar to special operations activities.

"(j) Special operations activities. For purposes of this section, special operations activities include each of the following insofar as it relates to special operations:

"(1) Direct action.

"(2) Strategic reconnaissance.

"(3) Unconventional warfare.

"(4) Foreign internal defense.

"(5) Civil affairs.

"(6) Military information support operations.

"(7) Counterterrorism.

"(8) Humanitarian assistance.

"(9) Theater search and rescue.

"(10) Such other activities as may be specified by the President or the Secretary of Defense."

D. Limitations

The statute imposed the limitation that funding for special operations activities did not constitute authority to conduct intelligence activities that would require congressional notice:

"(g) Intelligence and special activities. This section does not constitute authority to conduct any activity which, if carried out as an intelligence activity by the Department of Defense, would require a notice to the Select Committee on Intelligence of the Senate and the Permanent Select Committee on Intelligence of the House of Representatives under Title V of the National Security Act of 1947 (50 U.S.C. 413 et seq.)."[8]

E. The Definition of Major Force Program 2—General Purpose Forces

The DFAS-IN Manual defines general purpose forces in the following way:[9]

General purpose forces are those organizations and associated weapon systems whose force mission responsibilities are, at a given point in time, limited to one

---

[8] 10 U.S.C. § 167(g) (2013).

[9] DFAS-IN Manual 37-100-12, The Army Management Structure General Information OSD Program Component (FY2012-Change 3), August 31, 2011 at 14-OSDPG-1 to 14-OSDPG-2; additional guidance on the PPBE process was released January 25, 2013, in DoDD 7045.14, Planning Programming Budgeting and Execution (PPBE) Process.

theater of operations. Program 2 consists of Force-oriented program elements, including the command organizations associated with these forces, the logistic organizations organic to these forces, and the related support units that are deployed or deployable as constituent parts of military forces and field organizations. Also included are other programs, such as Joint Chiefs of Staff–directed and coordinated exercises, war reserve materiel ammunition and equipment, and stock-funded war reserve materiel.

Below we list and summarize other sources of funding that are being used or have been used in the past to fund SOF.

A summary of funding sources other than MFP-2 and MFP-11 is provided in Table B.1. A complete description of the source of funding, purpose, and limitations is included following Table B.1

Table B.1
Overview of Funding Sources

Source	Description	Purpose	Limitations
Global Security Contingency Fund (Pub. L. 112-81 § 1207, codified at 22 U.S.C. § 2151 note)	An account in the United States Treasury has been established called the "Global Security Contingency Fund." The Department of Defense may not contribute more than $200 million to this fund in any fiscal year; for any activity, the Secretary of Defense may contribute no more than 80% of the funds, and the Secretary of State may contribute no less than 20% of the funds.	"[T]o provide assistance to countries designated by the Secretary of State, with the concurrence of the Secretary of Defense, for purposes of this section, as follows: (1) To enhance the capabilities of a country's national military forces, and other national security forces that conduct border and maritime security, internal defense, and counterterrorism operations, as well as the government agencies responsible for such forces, to "(A) conduct border and maritime security, internal defense, and counterterrorism operations; and "(B) participate in or support military, stability, or peace support operations consistent with United States foreign policy and national security interests. "(2) For the justice sector (including law enforcement and prisons), rule of law programs, and stabilization efforts in a country in cases in which the Secretary of State, in consultation with the Secretary of Defense, determines that conflict or instability in a country or region challenges the existing capability of civilian providers to deliver such assistance." (22 U.S.C. § 2151(b)).	Assistance may be provided only for activities that promote "observance of and respect for human rights and fundamental freedoms" and "respect for legitimate civilian authority" (22 U.S.C. § 2151(c)). Funds will remain available until September 30, 2015; amounts set aside for activities that commenced before that date will be available to meet obligations that occur after that date. Security programs shall be jointly designed by the Secretary of State and the Secretary of Defense; justice sector and stabilization programs shall be designed by the Secretary of State "with the concurrence of the Secretary of Defense." (22 U.S.C. § 2151(d)) Assistance programs "shall be approved by the Secretary of State, with the concurrence of the Secretary of Defense." (22 U.S.C. § 2151(d)).

TableB.1—Continued

Source	Description	Purpose	Limitations
Cooperative Threat Reduction (50 U.S.C. § 2922)	This statute authorizes the appropriation of "such sums as may be necessary for fiscal year 2008" to • Destroy chemical weapons in Shchuch'ye, Russia • Prevent biological weapons proliferation • Allow the "[a]cceleration, expansion, and strengthening of Cooperative Threat Reduction Program activities" (50 U.S.C. § 2922(b))		Appropriated funds "may not exceed the amounts authorized to be appropriated by any national defense authorization act for fiscal year 2008 to the Department of Defense Cooperative Threat Reduction Program for such purposes." (50 U.S.C. § 2922(a)). Congress requests that the President "accelerate and expand funding" for these programs in future years. (50 U.S.C. § 2922(b)).
Emergency Extraordinary Expense Funds (10 U.S.C. § 127)	Funds may be authorized by the Secretary of Defense, the Inspector General of the Department of Defense, or the secretary of a Military Department within his Department.	May "provide for any emergency or extraordinary expense which cannot be anticipated or classified." (10 U.S.C. § 127(a))	The Secretary of Defense must notify certain congressional committees, and allow a certain period of time to pass before spending more than $500,000. This requirement is waived if the Secretary of Defense determines that compliance will compromise national security objectives; however, he then must notify the committees immediately.
Confidential Military Purpose Funds	Expenditures of Emergency Extraordinary Expense Funds may be authorized without disclosing their purpose, provided that the appropriate secretary or inspector general certifies that these expenditures are necessary for confidential military purposes.		Limitations are substantively the same as those for Emergency Extraordinary Expense Funds. Additionally, the appropriate secretary or inspector general must certify that the expenditure is necessary for confidential military purposes.

Table B.1—Continued

Source	Description	Purpose	Limitations
Joint Combined Exchange Training (10 U.S.C. § 2011)	The commander of the special operations command or of any other unified or specified combatant command may pay certain expenses incurred in the course of training with a friendly foreign country, including the expenses of the SOF, deployment expenses, and, if the friendly foreign nation is a developing nation, their incremental expenses directly incurred in the course of training	"The primary purpose of the training for which payment may be made . . . shall be to train the special operations forces of the combatant command." (10 U.S.C. § 2011(b))	The Secretary of Defense shall develop regulations related to this funding, including a requirement that funded activities must have the prior approval of the Secretary of Defense.
Combatant Commander Initiative Fund (10 U.S.C. § 166a)	Funds are drawn from the Combatant Commander Initiative Fund from the Department of Defense budget account by the Chairman of the Joint Chief of Staff	Funds may be used for: "(1) Force training. (2) Contingencies. (3) Selected operations. (4) Command and control. (5) Joint exercises (including activities of participating foreign countries). (6) Humanitarian and civic assistance, in coordination with the relevant chief of mission to the extent practicable, to include urgent and unanticipated humanitarian relief and reconstruction assistance. (7) Military education and training to military and related civilian personnel of foreign countries (including transportation, translation, and administrative expenses). (8) Personnel expenses of defense personnel for bilateral or regional cooperation programs. (9) Force protection. (10) Joint warfighting capabilities." (10 U.S.C. § 166a(b))	May not spend more than • $20 million on items "with a unit cost in excess of the investment unit cost." (10 U.S.C. §166 a(e)) • $10 million to pay expenses of foreign nations during joint exercises • $5 million to provide military education and training to personnel of foreign countries May not provide funds for "any activity that has been denied authorization by Congress."

Table B.1—Continued

Source	Description	Purpose	Limitations
Combat Mission Requirements Fund (10 U.S.C. § 167)	These funds "are amounts available to the Department of Defense for Defense-wide procurement in the Combat Mission Requirements subaccount of the Defense-wide Procurement Account." (10 U.S.C. § 167)		This section does not list any limitations, although there are extensive reporting requirements.
Commander's Emergency Response Program	Funds were originally derived from seized government assets during the occupation of Iraq; these assets were later supplemented with U.S. appropriations funds	To "respond to urgent humanitarian relief and reconstruction requirements within [the commanders'] areas of responsibility, by carrying out programs that will immediately assist the Iraqi people and support the reconstruction of Iraq" (June 16 memo by Ambassador Bremer)	"Frago 89 prohibited expenditures for seven categories: – direct or indirect benefit of CJTF-7 forces, to include coalition forces – entertaining Iraqi population – weapons buy-back or rewards programs – buying firearms, ammunition, or removing unexploded ordnance – duplicating services available through municipal governments – supporting individuals or private businesses (exceptions possible, such as repairing damage caused by coalition forces) – salaries for the civil work force, pensions, or emergency civil service worker payments" (37 JFQ 46, 48) The amounts that may be spent (both per transaction and in general) depends on the level of the commander authorizing the transaction.
Pub. L. 109-163 § 1206	Funds are drawn from the funds available for defense authorizations. This spending was originally authorized in 2006 but has been reauthorized every year since	"[T]o conduct or support a program to build the capacity of a foreign country's national military forces in order for that country to (1) conduct counterterrorist operations; or (2) participate in or support military and stability operations in which the U.S. Armed Forces are a participant." (Pub. L. 109-164, § 1206(a))	The Secretary of Defense must have the concurrence of the Secretary of State. Limited to $350 million in funds. Shall include elements that promote respect for human rights, fundamental freedoms, and legitimate civilian authority.

Table B.1—Continued

Source	Description	Purpose	Limitations
Pub. L. 108-375 § 1208	Funds are provided by the Secretary of Defense	"[T]o provide support to foreign forces, groups, or individuals engaged in supporting or facilitating ongoing military operations by United States special operations forces to combat terrorism." (Pub. L. 108-375 § 1208(a))	Before spending funds, the Secretary must establish procedures and inform Congress of these provisions. This authority cannot be delegated. This does not "constitute authority to conduct a covert action." (Pub. L. 108-375 § 1208(e))

2. Global Security Contingency Fund—Pub.L. 112-81 § 1207(a), codified at 22 U.S.C. § 2151 Note

A. Source

Summary

The Global Security Contingency Fund has been established as an account in the United States Treasury. Funds provided for this account may not exceed $350 million in fiscal year 2012 and $300 million in subsequent fiscal years.

- Of the FY 2012 funds, no more than $75 million may be used to increase the capacity of national military and security forces in certain African countries "to conduct counterterrorism operations against al-Qaeda, al-Qaeda affiliates, and al Shabaab."
- Of the FY 2012 funds, no more than $75 million may be used to "enhance the ability of the Yemen Ministry of Interior Counter Terrorism Forces to conduct counter-terrorism operations against al-Qaeda in the Arabian Peninsula and its affiliates."

DoD may not contribute more than $200 million to this fund in any fiscal year. The Secretary of State may contribute no less than 20 percent of the amount required for any activity; the Secretary of Defense may contribute no more than 80 percent.

Text of the Statute:

"There is established on the books of the Treasury of the United States an account to be known as the 'Global Security Contingency Fund' (in this section referred to as the 'Fund')." Pub. L. 112-81 § 1207(a), codified at 22 U.S.C. § 2151 note.

Funding:

"(1) Fiscal year 2012. The total amount available to the Department of Defense and the Department of State to provide assistance under this section during fiscal year 2012 may not exceed $350,000,000, of which—

"(A) $75,000,000 may be used for assistance authorized by subparagraphs (A) and (B) of subsection (n)(1); and

"(B) $75,000,000 may be used for assistance authorized by subparagraph (C) of subsection (n)(1).

"(2) Fiscal years 2013 and after. The total amount available to the Department of Defense and the Department of State to provide assistance under this section during a fiscal year after fiscal year 2012 may not exceed $300,000,000."

B. Purpose

- Funds may be used by either the Secretary of State or the Secretary of Defense to assist countries designated by the Secretary of State to:
  - Improve their military, security, and counterterrorism forces' ability to provide internal security, border security, and counterterrorism operations;
  - Engage in support operations "consistent with United States foreign policy and national security interests;"
  - Conduct justice sector, rule of law, and stabilization activities "in cases in which the Secretary of State, in consultation with the Secretary of Defense, determines that conflict or instability in a country or region challenges the existing capability of civilian providers."

Text of the Statute:

"(b) Authority. – Notwithstanding any other provision of law (other than the provisions of section 620A of the Foreign Assistance Act of 1961 (22 U.S.C. § 2371) and the section 620J of such Act relating to limitations on assistance to security forces (22 U.S.C. § 2378d)), amounts in the Fund shall be available to either the Secretary of State or the Secretary of Defense to provide assistance to countries designated by the Secretary of State, with the concurrence of the Secretary of Defense, for purposes of this section, as follows:

"(1) To enhance the capabilities of a country's national military forces, and other national security forces that conduct border and maritime security, internal defense, and counterterrorism operations, as well as the government agencies responsible for such forces, to—

"(A) conduct border and maritime security, internal defense, and counterterrorism operations; and

"(B) participate in or support military, stability, or peace support operations consistent with United States foreign policy and national security interests.

"(2) For the justice sector (including law enforcement and prisons), rule of law programs, and stabilization efforts in a country in cases in which the Secretary of State, in consultation with the Secretary of Defense, determines that conflict or instability in a country or region challenges the existing capability of civilian providers to deliver such assistance."

"(c) Types of assistance.

"(1) Authorized elements. A program to provide the assistance under subsection (b)(1) may include the provision of equipment, supplies, and training.

"(2) Required elements. A program to provide the assistance under subsection (b)(1) shall include elements that promote—

"(A) observance of and respect for human rights and fundamental freedoms; and

"(B) respect for legitimate civilian authority within the country concerned.

"(d) Formulation and approval of assistance programs.

"(1) Security programs. The Secretary of State and the Secretary of Defense shall jointly formulate assistance programs under subsection (b)(1). Assistance programs to be carried out pursuant to subsection (b)(1) shall be approved by the Secretary of State, with the concurrence of the Secretary of Defense, before implementation.

"(2) Justice sector and stabilization programs. The Secretary of State, in consultation with the Secretary of Defense, shall formulate assistance programs under subsection (b)(2). Assistance programs to be carried out under the authority in subsection (b)(2) shall be approved by the Secretary of State, with the concurrence of the Secretary of Defense, before implementation." Pub. L. 112-81 § 1207(b), codified at 22 U.S.C. § 2151 note.

C. Limitations

Summary

Only certain types of assistance may be funded:

- Must promote "observance of and respect for human rights and fundamental freedoms" and "respect for legitimate civilian authority."
- May include "provision of equipment, supplies, and training."

Security programs shall be jointly designed by the Secretary of State and the Secretary of Defense; justice sector and stabilization programs shall be designed by the Secretary of State "with the concurrence of the Secretary of Defense." Assistance programs "shall be approved by the Secretary of State, with the concurrence of the Secretary of Defense." In FY 2012, funds may be used to assist with "minor military construction," provided this assistance is not otherwise prohibited by law and is not given to a nation that is otherwise prohibited from receiving assistance.

- Such support may not be given to Yemen unless the Secretary of Defense and the Secretary of State certify that these activities are important to the United States' national security interests.
- This support must terminate before September 30, 2012, although funds available before that date may be used to conduct activities that are ongoing after that date.

Funds will remain available until September 30, 2015; amounts set aside for activities that commenced before that date will be available to meet obligations that occur after that date.

Text of the Statute:

"(c) Types of assistance.

"(1) Authorized elements. A program to provide the assistance under subsection (b)(1) may include the provision of equipment, supplies, and training.

"(2) Required elements. A program to provide the assistance under subsection (b)(1) shall include elements that promote—

"(A) observance of and respect for human rights and fundamental freedoms; and

"(B) respect for legitimate civilian authority within the country concerned.

"(d) Formulation and approval of assistance programs.

"(1) Security programs. The Secretary of State and the Secretary of Defense shall jointly formulate assistance programs under subsection (b)(1). Assistance programs to be carried out pursuant to subsection (b)(1) shall be approved by the Secretary of State, with the concurrence of the Secretary of Defense, before implementation."

"(2) Justice sector and stabilization programs. The Secretary of State, in consultation with the Secretary of Defense, shall formulate assistance programs under subsection (b)(2). Assistance programs to be carried out under the authority in subsection (b)(2) shall be approved by the Secretary of State, with the concurrence of the Secretary of Defense, before implementation." Pub. L. 112-81 § 1207(c), codified at 22 U.S.C. § 2151 note.

Funding limitations: "The total amount of funds transferred to the Fund in any fiscal year from the Department of Defense may not exceed $200,000,000." Pub. L. 112-81 § 1207(f)(2), 22 U.S.C. § 2151 note.

Allocation requirements: "The contribution of the Secretary of State to an activity under the authority in subsection (b) shall be not less than 20 percent of the total amount required for such activity. The contribution of the Secretary of Defense to such activity shall be not more than 80 percent of the total amount required." Pub. L. 112-81 § 1207(g), codified at 22 U.S.C. § 2151 note.

Availability limitations: "Amounts in the Fund shall remain available until September 30, 2015, except that amounts appropriated or transferred to the Fund before that date shall remain available for obligation and expenditure after that date for activities under programs commenced under subsection (b) before that date." Pub. L. 112-81 § 1207(i), codified at 22 U.S.C. § 2151 note.

Expiration: "The authority under this section may not be exercised after September 30, 2015. An activity under a program authorized by subsection (b) commenced before that date may be completed after that date, but only using funds available for fiscal years 2012 through 2015." Pub. L. 112-81 § 1207(q), codified at 22 U.S.C. § 2151 note.

Transitional authorities:

"(1) In general. The Secretary of Defense may, with the concurrence of the Secretary of State, provide the types of assistance described in subsection (c), and assistance for minor military construction, during fiscal year 2012 as follows:

"(A) To enhance the capacity of the national military forces, security agencies serving a similar defense function, and border security forces of Djibouti, Ethiopia, and Kenya to conduct counterterrorism operations against al-Qaeda, al-Qaeda affiliates, and al Shabaab.

"(B) To enhance the capacity of national military forces participating in the African Union Mission in Somalia to conduct counterterrorism operations described in subparagraph (A).

"(C) To enhance the ability of the Yemen Ministry of Interior Counter Terrorism Forces to conduct counter-terrorism operations against al-Qaeda in the Arabian Peninsula and its affiliates.

"(2) Limitations.

"(A) Assistance otherwise prohibited by law. The Secretary of Defense may not use the authority in this subsection to provide any type of assistance that is otherwise prohibited by any provision of law.

"(B) Eligible countries. The Secretary of Defense may not use the authority in this subsection to provide a type of assistance to a foreign country that is otherwise prohibited from receiving such type of assistance under any other provision of law.

"(C) Yemen. The authority specified in paragraph (1)(C), and the authority to provide assistance pursuant to section 1206 of the National Defense Authorization Act for Fiscal Year 2006 (Pub. L. 109-163; 119 Stat. 2456) [unclassified], may not be used for Yemen until 30 days after the date on which the Secretary of Defense and the Secretary of State jointly certify in writing to the specified congressional committees that the use of such authority is important to the national security interests of the United States. The certification shall include the following:

"(i) The reasons for the certification.

"(ii) A justification for the provision of assistance.

"(iii) An acknowledgment by the Secretary of Defense and the Secretary of State that they have received assurance from the Government of Yemen that any assistance so provided will be utilized in [a] manner consistent with subsection (c)(2)." Pub. L. 112-81 § 1207(n), codified at 22 U.S.C. § 2151 note.

3. Cooperative Threat Reduction—50 U.S.C. § 2922

A. Source
Summary

This statute authorizes the appropriation of "such sums as may be necessary for fiscal year 2008" to

- Destroy chemical weapons in Shchuch'ye, Russia
- Prevent biological weapons proliferation
- Allow the "[a]cceleration, expansion, and strengthening of Cooperative Threat Reduction Program activities."

Text of the Statute:

"[T]here are authorized to be appropriated to the Department of Defense Cooperative Threat Reduction Program such sums as may be necessary for fiscal year 2008 for the following purposes:

"(A) Chemical weapons destruction at Shchuch'ye, Russia.

"(B) Biological weapons proliferation prevention.

"(C) Acceleration, expansion, and strengthening of *Cooperative Threat Reduction*." 50 U.S.C. § 2922(a)(1)

B. Limitations
Summary

Appropriated funds "may not exceed the amounts authorized to be appropriated by any national defense authorization act for fiscal year 2008 to the Department of Defense Cooperative Threat Reduction Program for such purposes." Congress requests that the President "accelerate and expand funding" for these programs in future years.

Text of the Statute:

"The sums appropriated pursuant to paragraph (1) may not exceed the amounts authorized to be appropriated by any national defense authorization Act for fiscal year 2008 (whether enacted before or after the date of the enactment of this Act) to the Department of Defense Cooperative Threat Reduction Program for such purposes." 50 U.S.C. § 2922(a)(2)

"It is the sense of Congress that in fiscal year 2008 and future fiscal years, the President should accelerate and expand funding for Cooperative Threat

Reduction programs administered by the Department of Defense and such efforts should include, beginning upon enactment of this Act [enacted Aug. 3, 2007], encouraging additional commitments by the Russian Federation and other partner nations, as recommended by the 9/11 Commission." 50 U.S.C. § 2922(b)

4. Emergency Extraordinary Expense Funds—10 U.S.C. § 127

A. Source
Summary:
Funds may be authorized by

- The Secretary of Defense;
- The Inspector General of the Department of Defense;
- The Secretary of a Military Department within his Department.

Funds "may be spent on the approval or authority of the Secretary concerned or the Inspector General for any purpose he determines to be proper." The authority to release these funds may be delegated.

Text of the Statute:
"[T]he Secretary of Defense, the Inspector General of the Department of Defense, and the Secretary of a military department within his department, may provide for any emergency or extraordinary expense which cannot be anticipated or classified. When it is so provided in such an appropriation, the funds may be spent on approval or authority of the Secretary concerned or the Inspector General for any purpose he determines to be proper, and such a determination is final and conclusive upon the accounting officers of the United States. The Secretary concerned or the Inspector General may certify the amount of any such expenditure authorized by him that he considers advisable not to specify, and his certificate is sufficient voucher for the expenditure of that amount." 10 U.S.C. § 127(a)

B. Limitations
Summary
Funds over $500,000 may not be spent before the Secretary of Defense has notified the Committee on Armed Services and the Committee on Appropriations of both the House of Representatives and the Senate and a certain amount of time has passed.

- The waiting period to spend the funds depends on the amount to be spent. This requirement is waived if the Secretary of Defense determines that compliance will compromise national security objectives.
- In this case, he must notify the committees immediately.

Text of the Statute:

The authorizing agent must act "within the limitation of appropriations made for the purpose." 10 U.S.C. § 127(a)

"(1) Funds may not be obligated or expended in an amount in excess of $500,000 under the authority of subsection (a) or (b) until the Secretary of Defense has notified the Committee on Armed Services and the Committee on Appropriations of the Senate and the Committee on Armed Services and the Committee on Appropriations of the House of Representatives of the intent to obligate or expend the funds, and—

"(A) in the case of an obligation or expenditure in excess of $1,000,000, 15 days have elapsed since the date of the notification; or

"(B) in the case of an obligation or expenditure in excess of $500,000, but not in excess of $1,000,000, 5 days have elapsed since the date of the notification.

"(2) Subparagraph (A) or (B) of paragraph (1) shall not apply to an obligation or expenditure of funds otherwise covered by such subparagraph if the Secretary of Defense determines that the national security objectives of the United States will be compromised by the application of the subparagraph to the obligation or expenditure. If the Secretary makes a determination with respect to an obligation or expenditure under the preceding sentence, the Secretary shall immediately notify the committees referred to in paragraph (1) that such obligation or expenditure is necessary and provide any relevant information (in classified form, if necessary) jointly to the chairman and ranking minority member (or their designees) of such committees.

"(3) A notification under paragraph (1) and information referred to in paragraph (2) shall include the amount to be obligated or expended, as the case may be, and the purpose of the obligation or expenditure." 10 U.S.C. § 127(c)

5. Confidential Military Purpose Funds—Pub. L. 112-10, April 15, 2011[10]

A. Source

Summary

The Defense Secretary, Inspector General or a secretary of a MILDEP may spend Emergency Extraordinary Expense Funds without disclosure of their purpose. Department of Defense Appropriations Acts generally allow for funds "to be expended upon

---

[10] The National Defense Authorization Act for Fiscal Year 2013 does not contain similar provisions for "emergencies and extraordinary expenses" with payments made on the certificate of necessity of the secretary of a Service "for confidential military purposes."

the approval of the Secretary of the cognizant Military Service, and payments may be made on their certificate of necessity for confidential military purposes."[11]

Text of the Statute:
"PUBLIC LAW 112–10—APR. 15, 2011
OPERATION AND MAINTENANCE, ARMY
For expenses, not otherwise provided for, necessary for the operation and maintenance of the Army, as authorized by law; and not to exceed $12,478,000 can be used for emergencies and extraordinary expenses, to be expended on the approval or authority of the Secretary of the Army, and payments may be made on his certificate of necessity for confidential military purposes, $33,306,117,000.
OPERATION AND MAINTENANCE, NAVY
For expenses, not otherwise provided for, necessary for the operation and maintenance of the Navy and the Marine Corps, as authorized by law; and not to exceed $14,804,000 can be used for emergencies and extraordinary expenses, to be expended on the approval or authority of the Secretary of the Navy, and payments may be made on his certificate of necessity for confidential military purposes, $37,809,239,000.
OPERATION AND MAINTENANCE, AIR FORCE
For expenses, not otherwise provided for, necessary for the operation and maintenance of the Air Force, as authorized by law; and not to exceed $7,699,000 can be used for emergencies and extraordinary expenses, to be expended on the approval or authority of the Secretary of the Air Force, and payments may be made on his certificate of necessity for confidential military purposes, $36,062,989,000."

B. Limitations

Limitations are the same as Emergency Extraordinary Expense Funds (see details in previous section). The relevant secretary or inspector general must certify that the expenditure is necessary for confidential military purposes.

6. Joint Combined Exchange Training—10 U.S.C. § 2011

A. Source
Summary:
The commander of the special operations command or of any other unified or specified combatant command may pay

- Expenses incurred by the SOF "in conjunction with training, and training with, armed forces and other security forces of a friendly foreign country;"

---

[11] The National Defense Authorization Act for Fiscal Year 2013 does not contain similar provisions for "emergencies and extraordinary expenses" with payments made on the certificate of necessity of the secretary of a Service "for confidential military purposes."

- Deployment expenses related to the training;
- If training with a friendly developing country, "the incremental expenses incurred by that country as the direct result of such training."

Text of the Statute:

"Under regulations prescribed pursuant to subsection (c), the commander of the special operations command established pursuant to section 167 of this title [10 U.S.C. § 167] and the commander of any other unified or specified combatant command may pay, or authorize payment for, any of the following expenses:

"(1) Expenses of training special operations forces assigned to that command in conjunction with training, and training with, armed forces and other security forces of a friendly foreign country.

"(2) Expenses of deploying such special operations forces for that training.

"(3) In the case of training in conjunction with a friendly developing country, the incremental expenses incurred by that country as the direct result of such training." 10 U.S.C. § 2011(a)

B. Limitations

Summary

The "primary purpose" of the training must be to "train the special operations forces of the combatant command." The Secretary of Defense shall develop regulations related to this funding, including a requirement that funded activities have the prior approval of the Secretary of Defense.

Text of the Statute:

"The primary purpose of the training for which payment may be made under subsection (a) shall be to train the special operations forces of the combatant command." 10 U.S.C. § 2011(b)

7. Combatant Commander Initiative Fund—10 U.S.C. § 166a

A. Source

Summary:

Funds originate from the Combatant Commander Initiative Fund within the DoD budget account. The Chairman of the Joint Chiefs of Staff has authority to provide funds to a "commander of a combatant command" or an officer designated to receive funds for an area without a commander of a combatant command.

Text of the Statute:

"From funds made available in any fiscal year for the budget account in the Department of Defense known as the "Combatant Commander Initiative Fund", the Chairman of the Joint Chiefs of Staff may provide funds to the commander of a combatant command, upon the request of the commander, or, with respect to a geographic area or areas not within the area of responsibility of a commander of a combatant command, to an officer designated by the Chairman of the Joint Chiefs of Staff for such purpose." 10 U.S.C. § 166a(a)

B. Limitations

Summary

The commander of the special operations command or of any other unified or specified combatant command may pay

- Expenses incurred by the special operations forces "in conjunction with training, and training with, armed forces and other security forces of a friendly foreign country"
- Deployment expenses related to the training
- If training with a friendly developing country, "the incremental expenses incurred by that country as the direct result of such training."

Text of the Statute:

"(b) Authorized Activities.—Activities for which funds may be provided under subsection (a) are the following:

"(1) Force training.

"(2) Contingencies.

"(3) Selected operations.

"(4) Command and control.

"(5) Joint exercises (including activities of participating foreign countries).

"(6) Humanitarian and civic assistance, in coordination with the relevant chief of mission to the extent practicable, to include urgent and unanticipated humanitarian relief and reconstruction assistance.

"(7) Military education and training to military and related civilian personnel of foreign countries (including transportation, translation, and administrative expenses).

"(8) Personnel expenses of defense personnel for bilateral or regional cooperation programs.

"(9) Force protection.

"(10) Joint warfighting capabilities." 10 U.S.C. § 166a(b)

"(e) Limitations.—

"(1) Of funds made available under this section for any fiscal year—

"(A) not more than $20,000,000 may be used to purchase items with a unit cost in excess of the investment unit cost threshold in effect under section 2245a of this title [10 U.S.C. § 2245a];

"(B) not more than $10,000,000 may be used to pay for any expenses of foreign countries participating in joint exercises as authorized by subsection (b)(5); and

"(C) not more than $5,000,000 may be used to provide military education and training (including transportation, translation, and administrative expenses) to military and related civilian personnel of foreign countries as authorized by subsection (b)(7).

"(2) Funds may not be provided under this section for any activity that has been denied authorization by Congress." 10 U.S.C. § 166a(e)

8. Combating Terrorism Readiness Initiative Fund—10 U.S.C. § 166b

A. Source
Summary
Funds originate from the Combating Terrorism Readiness Initiatives Fund within the budget of DoD. Funds may be provided to the "commander of a combatant command" or an officer designated to receive funds for an area without a commander of a combatant command.

Text of the Statute:
"From funds made available in any fiscal year for the budget account in the Department of Defense known as the "Combating Terrorism Readiness Initiatives Fund", the Chairman of the Joint Chiefs of Staff may provide funds to the commander of a combatant command, upon the request of the commander, or, with respect to a geographic area or areas not within the area of responsibility of a commander of a combatant command, to an officer designated by the Chairman of the Joint Chiefs of Staff for such purpose." 10 U.S.C. § 166b(a).

B. Limitations
Summary
Funds may only be used for a specific list of activities, and may not be used for "any activity that has been denied authorization by Congress." Priority should be given to "emergency or emergent unforeseen high-priority requirements for combating terrorism."

Text of the Statute:
"**(b) Authorized activities.**—Activities for which funds may be provided under subsection (a) are the following:
"(1) Procurement and maintenance of physical security equipment.
"(2) Improvement of physical security sites.
"(3) Under extraordinary circumstances—
"(A) physical security management planning;
"(B) procurement and support of security forces and security technicians;
"(C) security reviews and investigations and vulnerability assessments; and
"(D) any other activity relating to physical security." 10 U.S.C. § 166b(b)
"**(c) Priority.**—The Chairman of the Joint Chiefs of Staff, in considering requests for funds in the Combating Terrorism Readiness Initiatives Fund, should give priority consideration to emergency or emergent unforeseen high-priority requirements for combating terrorism." 10 U.S.C. § 166b(c)
"**(e) Limitations.**—Funds may not be provided under this section for any activity that has been denied authorization by Congress." 10 U.S.C. § 166b(e)

9. Combat Mission Requirements Fund—10 U.S.C. § 167 Note[12]

A. Source
Summary
These funds "are amounts available to the Department of Defense for Defense-wide procurement in the Combat Mission Requirements subaccount of the Defense-wide Procurement Account."

Text of the Statute:
"Combat Mission Requirements funds are amounts available to the Department of Defense for Defense-wide procurement in the Combat Mission Requirements subaccount of the Defense-wide Procurement account." Pub. L. 11-383 § 123(a)(2), codified at 10 U.S.C. § 167 note.

B. Limitations
This section does not list any limitations, although there are extensive reporting requirements.

---

[12] Pub. L. 111-383 § 123, as amended by Pub. L. 112-81 § 145, codified at 10 U.S.C. § 167 note.

10. Commander's Emergency Response Program[13]

A. Source
Summary
Funds were originally derived from illicit government assets seized during the occupation of Iraq, which were later supplemented with U.S. funds. The initial goal of this program was to "respond to urgent humanitarian relief and reconstruction requirements . . . by carrying out programs that will immediately assist the Iraqi people and support the reconstruction of Iraq." (June 16 memo from Ambassador Bremer)

Detailed Summary:
Illicit assets seized during the occupation of Iraq were used to fund emergency public work projects. Funds seized were the property of the Iraqi government, rather than the private property of its citizens, in compliance with international law. According to a June 16 memo by Ambassador Bremer, as administrator of the Coalition Provisional Authority, these funds should be used to "respond to urgent humanitarian relief and reconstruction requirements within [the commanders'] areas of responsibility, by carrying out programs that will immediately assist the Iraqi people and support the reconstruction of Iraq." These funds may be used to purchase, among other things, "water and sanitary infrastructure, food production and distribution, healthcare, education, telecommunications, projects in furtherance of economic, financial, management improvements, transportation, and initiatives which further the rule of law and effective governance, irrigation systems installation or restoration, day laborers to perform civic cleaning, purchase or repair of civic support vehicles, and repairs to civic or cultural facilities" (FRAGO 89). Seized funds were later supplemented with funding through U.S. appropriations.

The National Defense Authorization Act for Fiscal Year 2013 provided a one-year extension for funding of the Commander's Emergency Response Program in Afghanistan. The amount of funding available for fiscal year 2013 was $200,000,000.

Text of the Statute:
"COMMANDERS' EMERGENCY RESPONSE PROGRAM IN AFGHANISTAN.

"(a) ONE-YEAR EXTENSION.—

"(1) IN GENERAL.—Section 1201 of the National Defense Authorization Act for Fiscal Year 2012 (Public Law 112–81; 125 Stat. 1619) is amended by striking "fiscal year 2012" each place it appears and inserting "fiscal year 2013".

---

[13] See Mark S. Martins, "The Commander's Emergency Response Program," *Joint Force Quarterly*, Issue 37, 2005, p. 46.

"(2) CONFORMING AMENDMENT.—The heading of subsection (a) of such section is amended by striking "FISCAL YEAR 2012"and inserting "FISCAL YEAR 2013".

"(b) AMOUNT OF FUNDS AVAILABLE DURING FISCAL YEAR 2013.—Subsection (a) of such section is further amended by striking "$400,000,000" and inserting "$200,000,000".[14]

B. Limitations

"FRAGO 89 prohibited expenditures for seven categories:[15]

- direct or indirect benefit of CJTF-7 forces, to include coalition forces;
- entertaining Iraqi population;
- weapons buy-back or rewards programs;
- buying firearms, ammunition, or removing unexploded ordinance;
- duplicating services available through municipal governments;
- supporting individuals or private businesses (exceptions possible, such as repairing damage caused by coalition forces);
- salaries for the civil work force, pensions, or emergency civil service worker payments."[16]

Restriction on payment of rewards was later relaxed. There are additional amount limits (both per-transaction and general spending ceilings) that depend on the level of the commander authorizing the transaction:

- Subordinate commanders can use standard forms for purchases up to $100,000.
- For purchases above $100,000, subordinate commanders must (1) inform the O-7/O-8 level commander in advance and (2) "obtain three competitive bids, identify a project manager, and pay for services as progress occurred."[17]

11. Pub. L. 109-163 § 1206

A. Source
Summary
This funding source was originally authorized in the FY 2006 National Defense Authorization Act but has been consistently reauthorized every year since. The Sec-

---

[14] Pub. L. 112-239 § 1221 (2013).

[15] Headquarters, Combined Joint Task Force 7, Fragmentary Order 89 (Commander's Emergency Response Program (CERP) Formerly the Brigade Commander's Discretionary Fund) to CJTF-7 OPORD 03-036 (192346 June 03) [hereinafter FRAGO 89].

[16] See Martins, 2005, pp. 46–48.

[17] See Martins, 2005, pp. 46–48.

retary of Defense, "with the concurrence of the Secretary of State," may use up to $350 million of funds available for defense operations "to conduct or support a program to build the capacity of a foreign country's national military forces" to enable that country to engage in counterterrorism operations or "participate in or support military or stability operations in which the United States Armed Forces are a participant."

Text of the Statute:

"The President may direct the Secretary of Defense to conduct or support a program to build the capacity of a foreign country's national military forces in order for that country to—(1) conduct counterterrorist operations; or (2) participate in or support military and stability operations in which the United States Armed Forces are a participant." (Pub. L. 109-163, § 1206(a))

B. Limitations
Summary

Limited to $350 million in funds. Must include elements that promote "human rights and fundamental freedoms" or "respect for legitimate civilian authority."

Text of the Statute:

"Required elements.—The program directed by the President under subsection (a) shall include elements that promote—(A) observance of and respect for human rights and fundamental freedoms; and (B) respect for legitimate civilian authority within that country." (Pub. L. 109-163, § 1206(b))

"(1) Annual funding limitation.—The Secretary of Defense may use up to $200,000,000 of funds available for defense-wide operation and maintenance for any fiscal year to conduct or support activities directed by the President under subsection (a) in that fiscal year. (2) Assistance otherwise prohibited by law.—The President may not use the authority in subsection (a) to provide any type of assistance described in subsection (b) that is otherwise prohibited by any provision of law. (3) Limitation on eligible countries.—The President may not use the authority in subsection (a) to provide assistance described in subsection (b) to any foreign country that is otherwise prohibited from receiving such type of assistance under any other provision of law." (Pub. L. 109-163, § 1206(c))

Pub. L. 109-163 § 1206—Subsequent Changes
Pub. L. 109-364 § 1206:

Program Implementation Vested in Secretary of Defense.—(1) Authority.— Subsection (a) of section 1206 of the National Defense Authorization Act for Fiscal Year 2006 (Pub. L. 109-163; 119 Stat. 3456) is amended by striking "The President may direct the Secretary of Defense to" and inserting "The Secretary of Defense, with the concurrence of the Secretary of State, may".

(2) Conforming amendments.—Such section is further amended—(A) in subsection (b), by striking "directed by the President" in paragraphs (1) and (2); (B) in subsection (c)—(i) in paragraph (1), by striking "directed by the President"; and (ii) in paragraphs (2) and (3), by striking "The President" and inserting "The Secretary of Defense"; (C) in subsection (d), by striking "directed by the President" both places it appears; and (D) in subsection (e)(2), by striking "as directed by the President". (b) Funding—Subsection (c)(1) of such section is further amended(1) by striking "$200,000,000" and inserting "$300,000,000"; and (2) by striking "defense-wide."

Pub. L. 110-181 § 1206:

"(a) Authority.—The Secretary of Defense, with the concurrence of the Secretary of State, is authorized during fiscal year 2008 to provide assistance to enhance the ability of the Pakistan Frontier Corps to conduct counterterrorism operations along the border between Pakistan and Afghanistan.(b) Types of Assistance.— (1) Authorized elements.—Assistance under subsection (a) may include the provision of equipment, supplies, and training. (2) Required elements.— Assistance under subsection (a) shall be provided in a manner that promotes— (A) observance of and respect for human rights and fundamental freedoms; and (B) respect for legitimate civilian authority within Pakistan. (c) Limitations.— (1) Funding limitation.—The Secretary of Defense may use up to $75,000,000 of funds available to the Department of Defense for operation and maintenance for fiscal year 2008 to provide the assistance under subsection (a). (2) Assistance otherwise prohibited by law.—The Secretary of Defense may not use the authority in subsection (a) to provide any type of assistance described in subsection (b) that is otherwise prohibited by any provision of law."

Pub. L. 110-417 § 1206:

"(a) Building of Capacity of Additional Foreign Forces.—Subsection (a) of sec-tion 1206 of the National Defense Authorization Act for Fiscal Year 2006 (Pub. L. 109-163; 119 Stat. 3456), as amended by section 1206 of the John Warner National Defense Authorization Act for Fiscal Year 2007 (Pub. L. 109-364; 120 Stat. 2418), is further amended by striking "a program" and all that follows and inserting "a program or programs as follows: (1) To build the capacity of a foreign country's national military forces in order for that country to— (A) conduct counterterrorism operations; or (B) participate in or support military and stability operations in which the United States Armed Forces are participating. (2) To build the capacity of a foreign country's maritime security forces to conduct counterterrorism operations.".(b) Funding.—Subsection (c) of such section, as so amended, is further amended—(1) in paragraph (1), by striking "$300,000,000" and inserting "$350,000,000"; and (2) by adding at the end the following new paragraph: "(4) Availability of funds for activities across fiscal years.—Amounts available under this subsection for the authority in subsection (a) for a fiscal year may be used for programs under that authority that begin in such fiscal year but end in the next fiscal year." (c) Three-Year Extension of Authority.—Subsection (g) of such section, as so amended, is further amended—(1) by striking "September 30, 2008" and inserting "September 30, 2011"; and (2) by striking "fiscal year 2006, 2007, or 2008" and inserting "fiscal years 2006 through 2011".

Pub. L. 111-81 § 1204:

- "(1) In general.—Subsection (c) of section 1206 of the National Defense Authorization Act for Fiscal Year 2006 (Public Law 109-163; 119 Stat. 3456), as most recently amended by section 1207(a) of the Ike Skelton National Defense Authorization Act for Fiscal Year 2011 (Public Law 111-383; 124 Stat. 4389), is further amended in paragraph (5) by striking "fiscal year 2012" and inserting "each of fiscal years 2012 and 2013"."
- "(c) One-year Extension of Authority.—Subsection (g) of such section, as most recently amended by section 1207(b) of the Ike Skelton National Defense Authorization Act for Fiscal Year 2011 (124 Stat. 4389), is further amended—(1) by striking "September 30, 2012" and inserting "September 30, 2013"; and (2) by striking "fiscal years 2006 through 2012" and inserting "fiscal years 2006 through 2013".

12. Pub. L. 108-375 § 1208

A. Source
Summary
The Secretary of Defense may spend up to $25 million "to provide support to foreign forces, irregular forces, groups, or individuals engaged in supporting or facilitating ongoing military operations by United States special operations forces to combat terrorism." (Pub. L. 108-375, § 1208(a))

Text of the Statute:
"(a) AUTHORITY.—The Secretary of Defense may expend up to $25,000,000 during any fiscal year during which this subsection is in effect to provide support to foreign forces, irregular forces, groups, or individuals engaged in supporting or facilitating ongoing military operations by United States special operations forces to combat terrorism.

"(b) PROCEDURES.—The Secretary of Defense shall establish procedures for the exercise of the authority under subsection (a). The Secretary shall notify the congressional defense committees of those procedures before any exercise of that authority.

"(c) NOTIFICATION.—Upon using the authority provided in subsection (a) to make funds available for support of an approved military operation, the Secretary of Defense shall notify the congressional defense committees expeditiously, and in any event in not less than 48 hours, of the use of such authority with respect to that operation. Such a notification need be provided only once with respect to any such operation. Any such notification shall be in writing."

References

United States Code

Pub. L. 99-661, National Defense Authorization Act for Fiscal year 1987.

Pub. L. 102-190, National Defense Authorization Act for Fiscal Years 1992 and 1993, December 5, 1991. As of March 7, 2014:
http://www.gpo.gov/fdsys/pkg/PLAW-104publ106/pdf/PLAW-104publ106.pdf

Pub. L. 108-375 § 1208, October 28, 2004. As of March 5, 2014:
http://www.gpo.gov/fdsys/pkg/PLAW-108publ375/pdf/PLAW-108publ375.pdf

Pub. L. 109-163 § 1206, NationL Defense Authorization Act for Fiscal Year 2006. As of March 5, 2014:
http://www.gpo.gov/fdsys/pkg/PLAW-109publ163/html/PLAW-109publ163.htm

Pub.L. 109-364, John Warner National Defense Authorization Act for Fiscal Year 2007. As of March 7, 2014:
http://www.gpo.gov/fdsys/pkg/PLAW-109publ364/pdf/PLAW-109publ364.pdf

Pub. L. 110-181, National Defense Authorization Act for Fiscal Year 2008 . As of March 7, 2014:
http://beta.congress.gov/110/plaws/publ181/PLAW-110publ181.pdf

Pub. L. 110-417, Duncan Hunter National Defense Authorization Act for Fiscal Year 2009. . As of March 7, 2014:
http://www.gpo.gov/fdsys/pkg/PLAW-110publ417/pdf/PLAW-110publ417.pdf

Pub. L. 111-383 § 1207, January 7, 2011. As of March 5, 2014:
http://www.gpo.gov/fdsys/pkg/PLAW-111publ383/html/PLAW-111publ383.htm

Pub. L., 112-81. National Defense Authorization Act for Fiscal Year 2012. As of March 7, 2014:
http://www.gpo.gov/fdsys/pkg/PLAW-112publ81/html/PLAW-112publ81.htm

Pub. L. 112-81, Veterans Health Care Budget Reform and Transparency Act of 2009, October 22, 2009. As of March 7, 2014:
http://www.gpo.gov/fdsys/pkg/PLAW-111publ81/pdf/PLAW-111publ81.pdf

Pub. L. 112-239, National Defense Authorization Act for Fiscal Year 2013 . As of March 7, 2014:
http://www.gpo.gov/fdsys/pkg/PLAW-112publ239/html/PLAW-112publ239.htm

Title 10 U.S.C.—Armed Forces (as amended through January 7, 2011), Vol. III, Subtitles B–E (§§ 3001–end). As of March 6, 2014:
http://www.gpo.gov/fdsys/pkg/CPRT-112HPRT67344/pdf/CPRT-112HPRT67344.pdf

Title 10 U.S.C. §§ 161–167 (a), Unified Combatant Command for Special Operations Forces, 2013. As of March 7, 2014:
http://www.gpo.gov/fdsys/granule/USCODE-2012-title10/USCODE-2012-title10-subtitleA-partI-chap6-sec167/content-detail.html

Title 22 U.S.C. § 2151, Foreign Relations and Intercourse, Congressional Findings and Declaration of Policy. As of March 7, 2014:
http://codes.lp.findlaw.com/uscode/22/32/I/I/2151

Title 22 U.S.C. § 2371, Foreign Assistance Act of 1961, Prohibition on Assistance to Governments Supporting International Terrorism. As of March 7, 2014:
http://codes.lp.findlaw.com/uscode/22/32/III/I/2371

Title 50 U.S.C. §§ 1621, 1631, and 1641 (2013).

Title 50 U.S.C. § 2922, Authorization of Appropriations for the Department of Defense Cooperative Threat Reduction Program . As of March 7, 2014:
http://codes.lp.findlaw.com/uscode/50/43/II/2922#sthash.ITlXFoBp.dpuf

Department of Defense Documents

Assistant Secretary of Defense for Special Operations/Low-Intensity Conflict and Interdependent Capabilities, ASD SO/LIC Memo, July 10, 1992.

Atwood, Donald, Guidance for Developing and Implementing Special Forces Program and Budget, 1 December 1989, memorandum to the Secretaries of the Military Departments, the Chairman of the Joint Chiefs of Staff, Under Secretaries of Defense, Assistant Secretaries of Defense, Comptroller, Commander-in-Chief United States Special Operations Command, and the Director of Administration and Management, December 1, 1989.

Carter, Ashton, Under Secretary of Defense, letter to CDR USSOCOM Admiral McRaven, February 6, 2012.

Defense Finance and Accounting Service 7900.4-M, *Financial Management Systems Requirements Manual*, Vol. 20, *Working Capital Funds*, September 2011.

Department of Defense, *Sustaining U.S. Global Leadership: Priorities for 21st Century Defense*, Washington, D.C., January 2012.

Department of Defense Directive DoDD 5100.03, Support of Combatant Commands and Subordinate Joint Commands, February 2, 2011.

Department of Defense Directive DoDD 5100.01, Functions of the Department of Defense and Its Major Components, December 21, 2010.

Department of Defense Directive DoDD 5100.3, Support of the Headquarters Combatant and Subordinate Joint Commands, November 15, 1999 (canceled).

Department of Defense Directive DoDD 7045.14, Planning Programming Budgeting and Execution (PPBE) Process, January 25, 2013.

Department of Defense Directive DoDD 5000.71, Rapid Fulfillment of Combatant Commander Urgent Operational Needs, August 24, 2012.

Department of Defense Instruction DoDI 4000.19, Interservice and Intergovernmental Support, August 9, 1995.

Department of Defense Instruction DoDI 5000.02, Operation of the Defense Acquisition System, November 26, 2013.

DFAS-IN Manual 37-100-12, *The Army Management Structure General Information OSD Program Component (FY2012-Change 3)*, August 31, 2011, at 14-OSDPG-1 to 14-OSDPG-3.

DoD 7000.14-R, Vol. 2B, Chap. 9, "Defense Working Capital Funds Activity Group Analysis," October 2008.

DoD Financial Management Regulation 7000.14-R, Vol. 3, Chap. 19, "Working Capital Funds," October 2008.

DoD FY 2010, Budget Request Summary Justification, Overseas Contingency Operations, May 2009.

Under Secretary of Defense (Comptroller), Memorandum, February 9, 1996.

Joint Publications

Joint Publication 1, Doctrine for the Armed Forces of the United States, May 2, 2007, Incorporating Change 1. March 20, 2009.

Joint Publication 1-02, *DOD Dictionary of Military and Associated Terms*, November 8, 2010, as amended through June 15, 2013.

Joint Publication 1-06, *Financial Management Support in Joint Operations*, March 2, 2012.

Joint Publication 3-22, Foreign Internal Defense.

Joint Publication 3-40, Chap. III, "Combating Weapons of Mass Destruction," November 2009.

Joint Publication 3-26, Chap. IV, "Counterterrorism."

Office of the Undersecretary of Defense (Comptroller), web site, undated. As of January 15, 2014: http://comptroller.defense.gov

USSOCOM Materials

USSOCOM, *The Global SOF Network*, March 22, 2012.

USSOCOM Briefing, "2006 Unfinance (sic) Requirements (UFRs) MFP-11 and MFP-2" (data reflect years 2006–2012).

USSOCOM Budget Estimates (FY 2010, 2011, 2012, 2013).

USSOCOM Directive 1-7, February 9, 2012.

USSOCOM Memorrandum of Understanding with the Department of the Army, August 17, 2011.

USSOCOM Memorrandum of Understanding with the Department of the Army, Annex E, "Administrative, Logistics and Installation Base Support Services," August 17, 2011.

USSOCOM Memorrandum of Understanding with the Department of the Navy, March 18, 2010.

United States Special Operations Command Operations and Maintenance, Defense-Wide Fiscal Year (FY) 2011 Budget Estimates.

United States Special Operations Command Operations and Maintenance, Defense-Wide Fiscal Year (FY) 2013 Budget Estimates.

USSOCOM SOFM-BD Points of Contact GCCs August 1, 2012.

USSOCOM SOFM-BD Spreadsheets, MFP11 Req MFP2 Other; 2006–2012 UFRs Final, July 25, 2012.

USSOCOM SOFM-BD TSOC Points of Contact July 25, 2012.

USSOCOM SOFM-MC, Recent Examples (of disputed funding sources), email excerpt, undated.

Woods, S. George, Director of Integration, USSOCOM Briefing, "Theater Special Operations Commands (TSOC) Resourcing Issues," July 20, 2011.

USCENTCOM Materials

USCENTCOM Crisis Response Element EXORD, DTG 132350Z, July 2011.

SOCCENT Materials

CFSOCC J-4 briefing, "CRE Logistics/Engineering Update," November 5, 2011.

Memorandum from SOCCENT Crisis Response Element to NSWU-3/JSOTF-GCC, Subject: SOCCENT CRE IOC CPX After Action Report, August 24, 2011.

SOCCENT CRE Master Plan, May 24, 2011.

SOCCENT CRE White Paper, December 30, 2011.

Congressional Testimony/Statements

Prepared statement by Linda Robinson, Adjunct Senior Fellow for U.S. National Security and Foreign Policy, Council on Foreign Relations, Before the House Committee on Armed Services, Subcommittee on Emerging Threats and Capabilities, United States House of Representatives, 2nd Session, 112th Congress, Hearing on the Future of Special Operations Forces, July 11, 2012.

Statement of Christopher J. Lamb, Distinguished Research Fellow, Center for Strategic Research, Institute for National Strategic Studies, National Defense University, on the Future of U.S. Special Operations Forces Before the Subcommittee on Emerging Threats and Capabilities, House Armed Services Committee, U.S. House of Representatives, July 11, 2012.

Statement for the record on U.S. SOCOM and SOF Futures Offered by Dr. Jacquelyn K. Davis Before the U.S. Congress House of Representatives Committee on Armed Forces Subcommittee on Emerging Threats and Capabilities, Hearing, July 11, 2012.

Department of the Army

Headquarters, Department of the Army, DA Memo 10-1, Organization and Functions, Executive Agent Responsibilities Assigned to the Secretary of the Army, January 15, 1997.

U.S. Army Special Operations Command Briefing Chart, Force Requirements GPF SPCs Request, undated.

Other Sources

Anderson, Wayne W., Jr., *Alternative Headquarters Support Funding for Theater Special Operations Commands*, Naval Postgraduate School, Monterey, Calif., thesis, December 2002.

Bremer, Paul, memo, June 16, 2003.

Chairman, Joint Chiefs of Staff Instruction 4320.01, Enclosure A, paragraph 1(a).

Commander, Combined Joint Task Force, CJTF-7, Fragmentary Order 89, June 19, 2003.

Defense Acquisition University, ACQuipedia, "Future Years Defense Program (FYDP)," web page, undated. As of January 14, 2014:
https://dap.dau.mil/acquipedia/Pages/ArticleDetails.aspx?aid=a2cc2ade-6336-433e-a088-42f497cdf7ef

Government Accountability Office, *Overseas Contingency Operations: Funding and Cost Reporting for the Department of Defense,* GAO-10-288R, December 18, 2009. As of February 22, 2014:
http://www.gao.gov/assets/100/96507.html

Headquarters, Combined-Joint Task Force 7, Fragmentary Order (FRAGO) 89, Commander's Emergency Response Program (CERP), formerly the Brigade Commander's Discretionary Fund) to CJTF-7 OPORD 03-036 (192346 June 03).

Jones, CAPT Mike, "Theater Special Operations Command Resourcing," TSOC Desk Officer briefing, USSOCOM, undated.

Martins, Mark S., "The Commander's Emergency Response Program," *Joint Force Quarterly,* Issue 37, 2005, pp. 46–48.

Stimson Center, "DoD Authorities for Foreign and Security Assistance Programs: A Comparison of the FY 2010 House and Senate Armed Services Defense Authorization Bills," July 20, 2009.

Szayna, Thomas S., and William Welser IV, *Developing and Assessing Options for the Global SOF Network,* Santa Monica, Calif.: RAND Corporation, RR-340-SOCOM, 2013. As of January 17, 2014:
http://www.rand.org/pubs/research_reports/RR340.html

U.S. Congress, Defense Conference Report, H. Rept. 102-311 pursuant to National Defense Authorization Act for Fiscal Years 1992 and 1993, Pub. L. 102-190, 1991. As of March 7, 2014:
http://beta.congress.gov/bill/102nd-congress/house-bill/2100